LEAD
TOEFL iBT
WRITING

LEAD
TOEFL iBT
WRITING

초판1쇄	2021년 04월 01일
개정판1쇄	2023년 05월 15일

지은이	DAVID CHIN
번　역	김슬기 박현욱 김은영 박영지
디자인	최주호(PETER CHOI)
펴낸이	박영은
펴낸곳	리드에듀북스
등록번호	395-91-01356
전　화	02-518-7776
팩　스	0504-489-4844
이메일	leadedubooks@naver.com
홈페이지	https://leadedubooks.modoo.at
저작권자	DAVID CHIN, 리드에듀북스

Photo Credit ⓒShutterstock.com

ISBN　979-11-973714-5-5　13740

이 책의 저작권은 저자와 출판사에 있습니다.
저작권자와 출판사의 허락없이 책의 일부 또는 전재 및 복제, 발췌하는 것을 금합니다.

낙장 및 파본은 구매처에서 교환해 드립니다.

값 19,900 원

PREFACE

　토플을 공부하는 학생들의 대부분은 교재의 선택권이 한정되어 있습니다. 점수 향상을 위해서는 다양한 지문을 읽고 수많은 문제를 풀어보아야 하지만, 선택권이 많지 않은 학생들은 불가피하게 비슷한 지문과 문제를 반복해서 풀 수밖에 없는 상황에 놓여 있습니다. 리드 토플은 이러한 상황이 개선되기를 바라는 학생들의 요구를 반영하여 만들어진 책입니다.

　저자인 저는 미국에서 초등, 중등, 고등 교육부터 대학 교육까지 받은 네이티브로서 영어-한국어 이중 언어 구사자입니다. 한국으로 귀국한 뒤 영어교육의 메카인 목동과 대치동에서 토플만을 전문적으로 강의하면서 다양한 강의 자료와 교수법을 직접 연구하고 개발하였으며 수업에 실제로 적용하였습니다. 그러한 과정에서 시중에는 존재하지 않는 새로운 교재 출간의 필요성을 느끼고 리드토플을 집필하였습니다.

　이 책은 기초를 다질 수 있는 연습 문제를 비롯하여, 높은 난이도의 실전 문제까지 세심한 주의를 기울여 설계된 문제들이 실려있습니다. 끊임없는 교재 개발과 연구를 바탕으로 한, 제가 가진 토플에 관한 모든 지식과 노하우가 담긴 책입니다.

　토플을 처음 접하는 학생, 혹은 영어 실력이 중급 수준인 학생들은 실전 문제집을 공부하는 것을 부담스럽게 느끼고 어려워합니다. 문제를 해결하는 스킬을 세심하게 알려주는 본 교재의 컨텐츠 디자인을 따라가면서 다양한 연습문제와 실전문제를 차근차근 풀어 나아간다면 자연스럽게 점수가 향상되는 경험을 하게 될 것입니다.

　앞으로도 풍성한 구성과 질 좋은 컨텐츠를 담아 지속적으로 출간될 리드 토플 교재가 여러분들의 토플 실력 향상에 커다란 밑거름이 되기를 소망합니다.

DAVID CHIN

LEAD TOEFL iBT WRITING

How to Use This Book

This book has been made to help new test takers understand the different essay questions first, then apply the writing templates to respond to the practice questions. After understanding and practicing the two different essays, test takers will then practice their writing in actual tests to further improve their skills and scores.

The writing section of the TOEFL test requires good note taking skills in order to write a good summary, and logic and explanation to write the opinionated essay. The essays all have time limits, so test takers should practice writing their essays within the given time.

The integrated essay is given 20 minutes to write a summary. The official TOEFL test will state 150-225 words for an adequate essay, but test takers should strive to write 300 words or more. The academic discussion essay is given 10 minutes to write an opinionated essay. The official TOEFL test will state 100 words for an adequate essay, but test takers should strive to write more than that.

Like any standardized test, it is best to achieve a top score by studying for the test within a minimal amount of time. Otherwise, the test taker will tire themselves out and eventually give up on their prospective score. The following chart is a tentative study plan for those who wish to achieve a high score on the TOEFL writing section.

LEAD TOEFL series all follow a 3 week study plan, so it is recommended that test takers use LEAD TOEFL Reading, Listening, and Speaking simultaneously while studying for the Writing section. The schedule has been balanced with the intention that test takers study for all four sections on a daily basis.

3 Week Study Plan

	Day 1	Day 2	Day 3	Day 4	Day 5
Week 1	Chapter 1 + Chapter 2 Practice 1	Chapter 2 Practice 2	Chapter 2 Practice 3	Chapter 2 Practice 4	Chapter 2 Practice 5
	Day 6	**Day 7**	**Day 8**	**Day 9**	**Day 10**
Week 2	Chapter 3 + Chapter 4 Practice 1	Chapter 4 Practice 2	Chapter 4 Practice 3	Chapter 4 Practice 4	Chapter 4 Practice 5
	Day 11	**Day 12**	**Day 13**	**Day 14**	**Day 15**
Week 3	Actual Test 1	Actual Test 2	Actual Test 3	Actual Test 4	Actual Test 5
	Official TOEFL Test				

If test takers are unable to finish their writing within the given time, they should increase their typing speed. Remember, just because you finished typing the last word for the essay when the timer is up, does not mean you finished on time. You failed to edit your essay!

Test takers must not look at the keyboard when typing and they should definitely not be typing with chopstick fingers. Try online typing games to make the practice more interesting.

About the TOEFL iBT

TOEFL (Test of English as a Foreign Language) iBT (Internet-Based Test) is an internet exam for students who speak English as a second language. The test is designed to assess a student's reading, listening, speaking, and writing abilities and how well they understand each section. Thus, the TOEFL test is divided into four sections: Reading, Listening, Speaking, and Writing.

Subject	Content	Time	Score
Reading	2 reading passages 10 questions per passage	36 minutes	0~30
Listening	2 conversations 5 questions per conversation 3 lectures 6 questions per lecture	36 minutes	0~30
Speaking	1 independent 3 integrated	16 minutes	0~30
Writing	1 integrated 1 academic discussion	30 minutes	0~30
		under 2 hours	0~120

About the TOEFL Writing Section

The TOEFL writing section is made up of two parts: the Integrated Writing Task and the Academic Discussion Task. The writing section analyzes the test taker's ability to organize and write the information clearly. The essays do not have to be creative. It needs to be clear and direct.

Integrated Writing Task:

This task consists of three parts. A reading passage, approximately 230 to 300 words in length, is given for 3 minutes. Next, a lecture that either agrees or disagrees with the reading will be presented. Finally, the test taker will be given 20 minutes to write a summary essay based on what they read and listened to. During this time, the reading passage will appear again. It is important to only write what test takers read and listened to, and not include any new information.

Academic Discussion Writing Task:

The last part of the entire TOEFL test is the academic discussion writing task. Test takers are given 10 minutes to state and support an opinion on a given topic in an online class discussion. A high scoring essay will have over 100 words. The response should be a contribution to the other two students' posts from an online discussion. Test takers should add their own perspective to the discussion and not simply repeat information that have already been mentioned.

Table of Contents

Chapter 1 – Integrated Essay Lesson   11

Chapter 2 – Integrated Essay Practices   27

Chapter 3 – Academic Discussion Lesson   69

Chapter 4 – Academic Discussion Practices   87

Actual Test 1   117

Actual Test 2   131

Actual Test 3   145

Actual Test 4   159

Actual Test 5   173

Answers and Script

CHAPTER 01
Integrated Essay Lesson

Integrated Essay

The objective of an integrated essay is to write a summary essay based on the notes the test taker took from the reading passage and the lecture. The essay should follow a structured format and should be able to summarize the major and minor ideas from the reading and the listening.

Before you start:

Draw a T-chart on your notebook and label "reading" on one side and "listening" on the other. Each side should have the main idea as well as three major points with space in between for minor ideas. The test taker should always take their notes in an organized manner.

The T-chart should look something like this:

READING	LISTENING
Main idea: _____	Main idea: _____
Major idea 1: _____	Major idea 1: _____
Major idea 2: _____	Major idea 2: _____
Major idea 3: _____	Major idea 3: _____

This T-chart can be simplified:

R	L
M: _____	M: _____
1: _____	1: _____
2: _____	2: _____
3: _____	3: _____

Reading notetaking:

The test taker will be given 3 minutes to read a passage and write down the main idea, major ideas, and minor ideas. Some test takers may not have enough time to write all this down. So, as soon as the timer starts and the reading passage comes out, their eyes should be focused on four lines from the reading passage.

Sample passage:

Humans and animals have lived alongside each other for many millennia. The former has achieved leaps and bounds in their individual rights as well as freedom in many different arenas. Animal rights have been ignored and will be continued to be rejected due to humans taking advantage of these lesser creatures. **[MAIN IDEA]**

[MAJOR IDEA 1] The primary advantage of humans using animals lie in pharmaceutical testing. Animals undergo drug testing so that the superior species can live a healthy and long life. Certain diseases and viruses are actually inflicted upon the animals and then treated with developing medicine so that humans can live a prosperous life. Without animal testing, new and developing drugs would have to be tested on humans, which many would refuse to participate for the sake of development. As such, animal rights must be ignored, so that mankind can become healthier.

[MAJOR IDEA 2] Another issue involves the displacement of wildlife due to industrial development. The human population grows at an exponential rate, so more housing and infrastructure is needed to accommodate the growing numbers. Thus, the space animals occupy on land and water are destroyed so that buildings and roads can be made. If animal rights are protected, then humans would have to live in cramped areas, which would be very uncomfortable and inconvenient.

[MAJOR IDEA 3] Finally, puppy mills and other underground operations provides cats and dogs to the average citizen at an affordable price. In recent years, the pet industry has increased in venue and specific breeds of cats and dogs are sought after at ludicrous costs. Although the animals are caged and do not receive the love and affection from a human owner, their offspring are sent to loving homes and grow in a healthy environment. Granting animal rights to these pets will deprive pet lovers from ever owning a cat or dog of their choice at an affordable price.

The test taker's notes should look something like this:

R	L
M: animal rights X b.c. humans taking adv	M: _____
1: pharm testing on animals animals tested → humans healthy diseases + virus inflict → treat w/ new med	1:_____
2: displace wildlife → indust develop human population↑→ need more housing + infra wildlife X so that buildings + road made	2:_____
3: puppy m. + underg. op. → cheap pets pet industry popular → sell pets $ animals caged and not receive love	3:_____

Notice that the notes are abbreviated and concise. Test takers should not use their time writing down sentences for their notes. Also, writing down minor ideas can be challenging for some test takers, so the order of notetaking should be as follows:

1) Main idea
2) Three major ideas

If there is time remaining, write down 2~3 details for each major idea.
If the test taker did not have enough time to write down the details, do not panic, the reading passage will appear again when you are writing the essay, so be sure to write down the details in your essay then.

It is important to write down the main idea and major ideas first because of the relationship between the reading passage and the lecture. In most cases, the lecture will argue against the points mentioned in the reading passage. So by understanding the reading's main idea and major points, one can guess what the lecture will discuss before even listening to it.

Listening notetaking:

Next, the test taker will be given a 2-minute lecture to listen and take notes. Unlike the reading passage, the lecture will only be played once, so it is important to write down as much you can, including the smallest details. This includes names and numbers.

Sample passage:

(CH1-Example.mp3)

The reading mentions that animal's rights have been ignored and will continue to be ignored because there are many benefits humans reap from them. However, the reading fails to notice that animal rights are actually being employed in the areas mentioned in its passage.

In regards to pharmaceutical testing, yes, the animals are treated with developing medicine which benefits humans and not the animals. However, the animal's well-being is considered as a priority during the testing. For example, when new drugs are administered to chimpanzees and they show the faintest signs of unwanted side effects, the chimps are given antibiotics and other approved medicine that help the animal to feel better. If animal rights were not considered, then the chimpanzee would have been left to die without any treatment.

Furthermore, when humans build roads and buildings in wildlife territory, they make sure that a part of the land is left untouched for the animals to retreat to and find haven. Construction companies are actually obligated by law to make infrastructure while leaving certain areas alone. Also, there are private groups that set up land and property for the homeless animals to make a new habitat. Thus, their rights to a home are actually being preserved while humans make their own homes to live in.

Lastly, the horrid condition of puppy mills and other underground operations were frowned upon by many people in the past. However, these days, puppy mills follow the conditions set up by animal right's activists that make sure the animals are in healthy and sanitary conditions. The animals in these mills are given play time to go outside and are fed with daily supplements the animal needs. At the same time, the offspring are given plenty of time to be nurtured by its mother before given off to a pet lover. So again, animal rights are preserved within puppy mills and other related facilities.

The test taker's notes should look something like this:

R	L
M: animal rights X b.c. humans taking adv	M: animal rights employed
1: pharm testing on animals animals tested → humans healthy diseases + virus inflict → treat w/ new med	1: animal's well-being - priority chimps tested w/ new drugs → unwanted side effect → treat if animal right X → left to die
2: displace wildlife → indust develop human population↑ → need more housing + infra wildlife X so that buildings + road made	2: build roads + bldgs, some land untouched obligated by law priv groups: set up land + property animal's rights to home preserved
3: puppy m. + underg. op. → cheap pets pet industry popular → sell pets $ animals caged and not receive love	3: puppy mills follow cond. by animal rights act. → healthy + sanitary play time outside + daily supplements offspring nurtured by mothers

Remember: take down as much details as you can. The more you write, the better it is. TOEFL integrated essay is graded on a relative scale, which means if you wrote something someone else could not, you will be given a higher score, while that person receives a lower score.

As you can see, the lecture notes contradict directly with what the reading passage mentions. On rare occasions, this relationship may be different. Some of these rare occasions include:

Casting Doubt

The example that was given was also a casting doubt format, however both the reading and the lecture focused on a single opinion (whether animal rights are protected or not). However, there are some cases where three different opinions may be given concerning a topic (ex: sturgeons jump for three purposes).

Problem and Solution

The reading passage will introduce a topic and present three problems. In contrast, the lecturer will propose three solutions for each of the problems.

Integrated Essay Template:

Introduction

The reading passage explains that (Reading's main idea).
However, the listening passage argues that (Lecture's main idea).

Body 1

To begin with, the writer claims that (Reading's major idea 1 + details).
On the other hand, the speaker contradicts this claim by stating that
(Lecture's major idea 1 + details).

Body 2

Furthermore, the author mentions that (Reading's major idea 2 + details).
Conversely, the lecturer goes against this by stating that
(Lecture's major idea 2 + details).

Body 3

Moreover, the text argues that (Reading's major idea 3 + details).
On the contrary, the lecture challenges this argument by stating that
(Lecture's major idea 3 + details).

It is not essential to memorize this template word to word; however, the test taker must understand the organization of the essay.

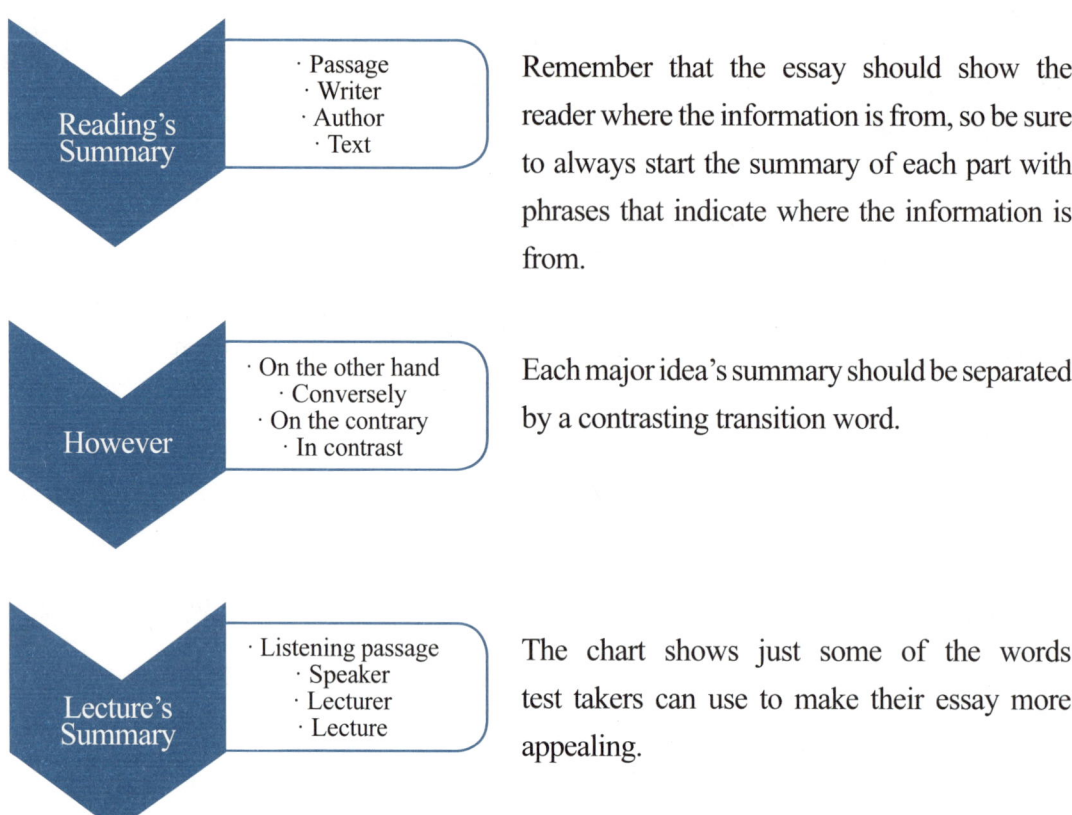

Remember that the essay should show the reader where the information is from, so be sure to always start the summary of each part with phrases that indicate where the information is from.

Each major idea's summary should be separated by a contrasting transition word.

The chart shows just some of the words test takers can use to make their essay more appealing.

Sample Essay:

The reading passage explains that animal rights are continuously being ignored due to humans taking advantage of them. However, the listening passage argues that animal rights are actually being protected.

To begin with, the writer claims that pharmaceutical products are being tested on animals and it infringes upon their rights. The testing is done on animals, not for their benefit, but for the sake of human health. Sometimes, the animals are injected with viruses or exposed to diseases and then treated with new medicine the pharmaceutical company is developing. On the other hand, the speaker contradicts this claim by stating that the animal's well-being is the number one priority for the pharmaceutical companies. For example, when the chimpanzees are tested with new drugs and show unwanted side effects, they are given treatments immediately to treat the pain. If animal rights were being ignored, the animals being tested on would have been left to die.

Furthermore, the author mentions that humans are displacing wildlife habitat for industrial development. As the human population is continuously increasing, they need more housing and infrastructure to accommodate their growing numbers. Animals are being ignored so that man can make more buildings and roads. Conversely, the lecturer goes against this by stating that some of the lands are left untouched while constructing roads and buildings. Construction companies are actually obligated by law to leave parts of the land untarnished. Also, private groups set up land and property for the animals that lost their homes. Thus, an animal's rights to a home are being preserved.

Moreover, the text argues that puppy mills and other related underground operations offer cheap pets to those wishing to own a pet. Recently, the pet industry has become popular and pets are being sold at high prices. The animals are caged and do not receive love, while they are forced to give birth to be sold at cheap prices. On the contrary, the lecturer challenges this argument by stating that puppy mills actually follow the conditions set by animal rights activists. The animals are housed in healthy and sanitary conditions. They are given time to play outside and fed with daily supplements. Also, the offspring are cared for by the mother before they are sold to pet owners.

376 words

On the official TOEFL test, the word count for the integrated essay is between 150-225 words. However, with the amount of notes taken, it is impossible to fit all the information within 225 words. Therefore, an essay recorded with all the major points, as well as the minor points from the reading and listening, should have a word count above 300 words. You will not be deducted points from writing a longer essay.

Remember, the test taker is given only 20 minutes to type the essay, so if your typing speed is slow, practice makes perfect. There are many online typing games to make the practice fun.

Do not forget to edit the essay. Editing is part of the essay writing process. Only when you finish editing when the timer goes off can you claim that you did a good job.

Why do you get a low score on the integrated essay?

1) Lack of information:

The purpose of an integrated essay is to summarize the reading and the listening. The test taker should provide both major and minor ideas, including small details like names and numbers.

2) Wrong information:

It is almost difficult to write wrong information from the reading since the passage appears next to the space where the test taker writes their essay. Wrong information comes from the lecture, where the test taker misheard certain information and wrote down something wrong.

3) New information:

Sometimes test takers tend to write down information that was not mentioned in the reading or the listening. Do not include information you may have from background knowledge.

4) Copying word to word:

Do not copy the reading passage. Paraphrase the information by using synonyms and changing the sentence structure.

5) Organization:

Remember that the organization of the essay should be reading first, then a contrasting word, and followed by the listening summary.

6) Typos and grammar mistakes:

One of the most frustrating mistakes test takers can make is misspelling a word. However, this is unforgiveable since the word that they write down appears in the passage next to the writing section. Grammar mistakes are actually hard to identify since someone who is poor in grammar will not be able to identify their mistake.

Vocabulary:

integrated	adj.	with various parts or aspects linked or coordinated.	*combined, consolidated*
format	n.	a defined structure for the processing, storage, or display of data.	*form, style*
millennia	n.	an anniversary of a thousand years.	
former	adj.	denoting the first or first mentioned of two people or things.	*first*
reject	v.	dismiss as inadequate, inappropriate, or not to one's taste.	*refuse, decline*
undergo	v.	experience or be subjected to (something, typically something unpleasant, painful, or arduous).	*experience, undertake*
superior	adj.	higher in rank, status, or quality.	*senior, higher*
inflict	v.	cause (something unpleasant or painful) to be suffered by someone or something.	*impose, force*
prosperous	adj.	successful in material terms; flourishing financially.	*thriving, flourishing*
sake	n.	for the purpose of; in the interest of; in order to achieve or preserve.	*purpose, reason, goal*
displacement	n.	the moving of something from its place or position.	*move, shift*
industrial	adj.	relating to or characterized by industry.	*business, factory*
exponential	adj.	(of an increase) becoming more and more rapid.	*growing, expanding*
accommodate	v.	(of physical space, especially a building) provide lodging or sufficient space for.	*house, board*
cramped	adj.	feeling or causing someone to feel uncomfortably confined or hemmed in by lack of space.	*confined, restricted*
underground	adj.	relating to the secret activities of people working to subvert an established order.	*secret, private*
venue	n.	the place where something happens, especially an organized event such as a concert, conference, or sports event.	*setting, site*
ludicrous	adj.	so foolish, unreasonable, or out of place as to be amusing; ridiculous.	*absurd, ridiculous*
offspring	n.	an animal's young.	*progeny, baby*

deprive	v.	deny (a person or place) the possession or use of something.	*strip, relieve*
reap	v.	cut or gather (a crop or harvest).	*harvest, garner*
employed	v.	make use of.	*utilize, use*
priority	n.	a thing that is regarded as more important than another.	*precedence, seniority*
administered	v.	dispense or apply (a remedy or drug).	*provide, issue*
faint	adj.	(of a sight, smell, or sound) barely perceptible.	*obscure, indistinct*
retreat	v.	withdraw to a quiet or secluded place.	*retire, withdraw*
haven	n.	a place of safety or refuge.	*refuge, shelter*
obligated	v.	bind or compel (someone), especially legally or morally.	*compel, require*
infrastructure	n.	the basic physical and organizational structures and facilities (e.g. buildings, roads, power supplies) needed for the operation of a society or enterprise.	
horrid	adj.	very unpleasant or disagreeable.	*horrible, unpleasant*
supplement	n.	a substance taken to remedy the deficiencies in a person's diet.	
nurture	v.	care for and encourage the growth or development of.	*take care, bring up*

Additional vocabulary:

CHAPTER 02

Integrated Essay Practices

Practice 1

These days, individuals seek venue in the free market system. Free market economists believe that a market where government interference is minimal, almost non-existent, is the most beneficial for both individuals and the governing body. There are three factors that prove free market capitalism is the favorable choice.

Free market capitalism has proven to be stable in many countries. For example, in the United States, the free market system has endured despite the economic downturns the country faced, especially during the Great Depression. Government bodies made poor choices in dealing with the economic difficulties, and only the free market capitalists witnessed no fluctuation in their business. Individuals are quick to act in cases of emergency so that they do not suffer any profit loss. Through this swift response, free market capitalists have remained strong in many different countries.

In a free market system, individuals, regardless of ethnicity or background, have the same opportunity to succeed in their economic venture. Successful accounts have proven that anyone can succeed. Mark Zuckerberg, the founder of Facebook, and the late Steve Jobs who made Apple into an electronics titan, both came from humble backgrounds and achieved success with their ideas and business. If the government had been involved in their affairs, the people would not have the social network connection nor the aesthetically designed gadgets we enjoy. So, a government free market allows anyone to be successful in their respective fields.

Lastly, government involvement in the economy is actually what causes the business cycle, which is an economic term for booms and busts within the business world. When the government misallocates resources towards businesses that do not respond to the demands of the consumers or are not sustainable in the long run, it actually creates market instability and creates the notorious business cycle.

Reading Notetaking

Reading	Listening
Main: Free Mkt Cap ☺ b/c 3 factors	
1. _____ - U.S.A, free mkt endure G.D. - Govt make poor econ choices - Indv quick to act → x profit loss	
2. _____ - Ex: Mark Z. + Steve J. - If govt involve → x SNS + x gadgets	
3. _____ - Govt misallocates resources → mkt instable - Result in business cycle	

Remember!
- Do not write complete words or sentences when you are taking notes.
- You only have 3 minutes to read and take notes. Write the main idea and the three major ideas first.
- If you have time, go ahead and write two or three details for each major idea.
- Don't worry if you are unable to write down all the details, the reading passage will appear again when you are writing your essay.

(CH2-1.mp3)

Listening Notetaking

Reading	Listening
Main: Free Mkt Cap ☺ b/c 3 factors	Main: Govt is most appr for mkt, x free enter
1. _____ - U.S.A, free mkt endure G.D. - Govt make poor econ choices - Indv quick to act → x profit loss	1. _____ - Other countries: govt involve partially - Govt's goal: prosperity - Indiv: greedy + power thirsty → mkt collapse
2. _____ - Ex: Mark Z. + Steve J. - If govt involve → x SNS + x gadgets	2. _____ - Powerful stay powerful, weak stay weak - Those with money, make more money. - Govt involve = x $ or x background → succeed
3. _____ - Govt misallocates resources → mkt instable - Result in business cycle	3. _____ - Keynesians belief - Fiscal policy (tax/borrow/spend) - Monetary policy - Prevent business cycle

Remember!
- Do not write complete words or sentences when you are taking notes.
- You will only have one chance to listen to the lecture!
- Write down all the small details, including names and numbers.

Integrated Essay

The reading passage claims that free market capitalism is favorable because of three factors. However, the listening passage argues that the government is the most appropriate body to monitor markets, not a free market enterprise.

To begin with, the writer claims that _____
_____.

The United States was able to endure the Great Depression because it is based on a free market enterprise. In decision making, the government makes poor choices, which can hurt the economy while individuals are quick to act, so there will be no economic loss in times of trouble. On the other hand, the speaker contradicts this claim by stating that _____
_____.

Countries outside of the United States have markets where the government is partially involved. The government's goal is for the country to prosper. Meanwhile, individuals are greedy and power thirsty so they are likely to lead the market to collapse.

Furthermore, the author mentions that _____
_____.

Successful individuals, such as _____
_____.

If the government had been involved, _____
_____.

Conversely, the lecturer goes against this by stating that _____
_____.

The powerful _____
_____.

With government involvement, _____
_____.

Moreover, the text argues that _____
_____.

The government misallocates _____
_____.

This will result _____.

On the contrary, the lecture challenges this argument by stating that _____
_____.

The Keynesians believe that _____
_____.

This will help prevent _____.

Vocabulary:

interference	n.	the action of interfering or the process of being interfered with.	*intrusion, involvement*
minimal	adj.	of a minimum amount, quantity, or degree; negligible.	*minimum, least*
favorable	adj.	expressing approval.	*approving, commending*
stable	adj.	(of an object or structure) not likely to give way or overturn; firmly fixed.	*firm, solid, steady*
endure	v.	suffer (something painful or difficult) patiently.	*undergo, experience*
downturn	n.	a decline in economic, business, or other activity.	*decline, slump*
witness	v.	have knowledge of (an event or change) from personal observation or experience.	*observe, watch*
fluctuation	n.	an irregular rising and falling in number or amount; a variation.	*variation, alteration*
swift	adj.	happening quickly or promptly.	*rapid, sudden*
venture	n.	a risky or daring journey or undertaking.	*enterprise, undertaking*
titan	n.	a person or thing of very great strength, intellect, or importance.	
humble	adj.	having or showing a modest or low estimate of one's own importance.	*meek, submissive*
aesthetically	adv.	in a way that gives pleasure through beauty.	
allocate	v.	distribute (resources or duties) for a particular purpose.	*assign, grant*
sustainable	adj.	able to be maintained at a certain rate or level.	*viable, continuous*
notorious	adj.	famous or well known, typically for some bad quality or deed.	*infamous, scandalous*
appropriate	adj.	suitable or proper in the circumstances.	*suitable, proper*
partially	adv.	only in part; to a limited extent.	*partly*
prosper	v.	succeed in material terms; be financially successful.	*thrive, flourish*
gluttony	n.	habitual greed or excess in eating.	*greed*
ideal	adj.	satisfying one's conception of what is perfect; most suitable.	*perfect, absolute*
prestigious	adj.	inspiring respect and admiration; having high status.	*reputable, respected*
advocate	n.	a person who publicly supports or recommends a particular cause or policy.	*champion, supporter*
fiscal	adj.	relating to government revenue, especially taxes.	*tax, revenue*
recession	n.	a period of temporary economic decline during which trade and industrial activity are reduced, generally identified by a fall in GDP in two successive quarters.	*downturn, slump*

Sample Essay

The reading passage claims that free market capitalism is favorable because of three factors. However, the listening passage argues that the government is the most appropriate body to monitor markets, not a free market enterprise.

To begin with, the writer claims that free market capitalism has been practical in many countries. The United States was able to endure the Great Depression because it is based on a free market enterprise. In decision making, the government makes poor choices, which can hurt the economy while individuals are quick to act, so there will be no economic loss in times of trouble. On the other hand, the speaker contradicts this claim by stating that although the United States may profit from a free market system, the rest of the world do not share the same advantage. Countries outside of the United States have markets where the government is partially involved. The government's goal is for the country to prosper. Meanwhile, individuals are greedy and power thirsty so they are likely to lead the market to collapse.

Furthermore, the author mentions that individuals have the same chance of business success in a free market system. Successful individuals, such as Mark Zuckerberg and the late Steve Jobs, surfaced from humble backgrounds and attained great success with their ideas and businesses. If the government had been involved, the public would not have the social network and aesthetic electronics we enjoy today. Conversely, the lecturer goes against this by stating that government involvement is important for the sake of equal opportunities. The powerful stay powerful and the rich stay rich in our current society. With government involvement, people with no money or prestigious background can still find success in the business world.

Moreover, the text argues that government involvement actually causes a business cycle, also known as boom and bust. The government misallocates resources towards companies that do not answer to the consumers nor are they able to sustain their business in the long run. This will result in market instability and the infamous business cycle. On the contrary, the lecture challenges this argument by stating that business cycles can be prevented with government participation. The Keynesians believe that the government should manage the free markets through fiscal policy, like taxing, borrowing, and spending and monetary policy, such as printing money and setting the interest rate. This will help prevent business cycles and economic recessions.

399 words

Practice 2

Many schools and research institutions are starting to rely more on educational videos and recordings. While the traditional educators prefer to teach the lesson themselves using textbooks, the dependence on educational media is actually a positive trend.

Students tend to pay more attention with visual aid from media sources. The twenty first century is an era with visual implications in many different areas, including education. Students are more used to watching videos than reading textbooks. With visual aids, teachers can have a greater chance in capturing the attention of their students. Also, teachers will have an easier time explaining difficult concepts to their students through the use of charts and animation. This will help students understand better, which is a definite advantage that will help students advance in their education.

Also, educational media are much cheaper than teachers and textbooks. Hiring a teacher for a one-time lesson is several times more expensive than giving the lesson through an educational video. Also, textbooks can cost more than a hundred dollars, while an educational DVD can be less than ten dollars. Since schools can purchase only one copy of the DVD instead of purchasing for each classroom, the cost of education can be further minimized. Students and school are constantly on tight budget, and they are always requesting for government aid. By purchasing educational media, students and schools can save lots of money, which they can use to purchase other important items.

Finally, educational media will provide access to education to a wider group of students. Although countries like the United States benefit from universal education, third world countries like those in Asia and Africa do not have schools for children to attend. If these children were given access to educational media, then they would receive the education they need for their age in the comfort of their homes. No child would be left behind with the use of educational media.

Reading Notetaking

Reading	Listening
Main: Edu media _____	
1. _____ - Students are used to _____ - With vis aids, _____ - Easier time explaining _____	
2. _____ - Hiring a teacher _____ - While textbooks cost _____ - Schools can save $ by _____	
3. _____ - Third world countries do not _____ - If children given _____ - No child _____	

(CH2-2.mp3)

Listening Notetaking

Reading	Listening
Main: Edu media _____	**Main:** _____
1. _____ - Students are used to _____ - With vis aids, _____ - Easier time explaining _____	1. _____ - Lesson will be _____ - Textbook filled with _____ - Edu media designed to _____ - Not educate.
2. _____ - Hiring a teacher _____ - While textbooks cost _____ - Schools can save $ by _____	2. _____ - Edu media x cheap - _____ - _____ - _____
3. _____ - Third world countries do not _____ - If children given _____ - No child _____	3. _____ - Families with low $ X edu media - _____ - _____ - _____

Integrated Essay

The reading passage claims that educational media _____
_____.

However, the listening passage argues that _____
_____.

To begin with, the writer claims that _____
_____.

Students are used to _____
_____.

With visual aids, _____
_____.

So teachers will have an easier time explaining _____
_____.

On the other hand, the speaker contradicts this claim by stating that _____
_____.

Lessons will be _____
_____.

Textbooks are filled with _____
_____.

Educational media are designed to _____
_____.

Therefore, educational media will not educate the students.

Furthermore, the author mentions that _____
_____.

Hiring a teacher is _____
_____.

While textbooks cost _____
_____.

Schools can save money by _____.

Conversely, the lecturer goes against this by stating that _____
_____.

Educational media are actually not cheap. _____
_____.

Moreover, the text argues that _____
_____.

Third world countries do not _____
_____.

If children are given _____.

Then, no child _____.

On the contrary, the lecture challenges this argument by stating that _____
_____.

Families with low income will not have access to educational media. _____
_____
_____.

Vocabulary:

rely	v.	depend on with full trust or confidence.	*depend, count*
trend	n.	a general direction in which something is developing or changing.	*tendency, movement*
implication	n.	the action or state of being involved in something.	*involvement, connection*
minimize	v.	reduce (something, especially something unwanted or unpleasant) to the smallest possible amount or degree.	*reduce, decrease*
plethora	n.	a large or excessive amount of (something).	*excess abundance*
term	n.	a fixed or limited period for which something, e.g., office, imprisonment, or investment, lasts or is intended to last.	*period, time*

Additional vocabulary:

Sample Essay

The reading passage claims that educational media is a positive trend. However, the listening passage argues that educational media will never replace traditional classrooms.

To begin with, the writer claims that students pay more attention with help from visual aids. With visual aids, teachers can have a higher chance grabbing the attention of their students. So teachers will have an easier time explaining difficult ideas to their students by using charts and animations. Then students will understand the lesson better and they can further their education. On the other hand, the speaker contradicts this claim by stating that educational videos are limited by time. Lessons will be incomplete and miss important details, so students will have questions. Textbooks are filled with lots of information to answer any questions students may have. Educational media are designed to entertain, not educate. This means that the lessons will be simplified and not explain difficult concepts. Therefore, educational media will not educate the students.

Furthermore, the author mentions that educational media are much cost efficient than teachers and books. Hiring a teacher is several times more expensive than providing a lesson through an educational video. Schools can save money by utilizing educational media. Conversely, the lecturer goes against this by stating that educational media are actually not cheap. Although videos of movies are cheap, educational media are costly since learning in whatever format is costly and these media are made to help students succeed in life. Also, students would have to purchase a DVD player or a computer in order to have access to educational media, which are expensive to buy and fix if it breaks. Even if the educational videos are offered online, an internet access would be required, which needs to be paid on a monthly basis.

Moreover, the text argues that educational media will provide learning to a wider group of students. Third world countries do not have schools for children to learn. If children are given educational media, they would be educated according to their age. On the contrary, the lecture challenges this argument by stating that educational media will have a limitation in their audience. Families with low income will not have access to educational media. Some families in America do not own computers at home, and villages in Asia and Africa own only one television set or computer. Sadly, most children in third world countries are working in factories so they have no time to study. So even with educational media, the people who have access to it will be small.

423 words

Practice 3

For many years, music education has become part of the American school curriculum. Some educational experts believe that all students should continue to study music. However, there are those who believe that mandatory music classes bring about a few problems.

First, music classes do not prepare students for a realistic career in society. The majority of students will pursue careers in science, business, or technology. Whatever students learn in music classes will not help them in their future careers. The purpose of attending school is to learn information and gain experience which will assist them later in life. Mathematic courses, science courses, and the like provide valuable information to students that can be practical in life. Thus, students should not take music classes since the classes do little to help them in their future careers.

Second, assessing students and giving them grades is unfair in these classes. There are some students who naturally have no talent in music. Sometimes they can be tone deaf. Although some people might say practice makes perfect, there are some cases where years of practice will not result in perfection. These students are likely to fail in music classes, while those who are naturally gifted in music will succeed. Since school grades are essential in order to get into a good university or even get a job, a failed mark in the student's report card will not help them at all.

Third, musical instruments are expensive. A violin can cost several hundred dollars, and a flute or clarinet can equally be expensive as well. For students who come from low income families, purchasing such expensive instruments can be a burden. Also, maintaining the instruments are costly as well. Violin strings must be changed after a few months of use and reeds used in clarinets must be replaced after a few weeks. The cost for repairing the instruments if they get damaged cannot be ignored as well.

Reading Notetaking

Reading	Listening
Main: Mandatory music classes _____	
1. _____ 　- Majority pursue science, business, or tech 　　- _____ 　　- _____ 　　- _____	
2. _____ 　- Some students have no natural talent in music 　　- _____ 　　- _____ 　　- _____	
3. _____ 　- Violin, flute, clarinet $ 　　- _____ 　　- _____ 　　- _____	

(CH2-3.mp3)

Listening Notetaking

Reading	Listening
Main: Mandatory music classes _____	**Main:** _____
1. _____ - Majority pursue science, business, or tech - _____ - _____ - _____	1. _____ - Music class stimulate other classes - _____ - _____ - _____
2. _____ - Some students have no natural talent in music - _____ - _____ - _____	2. _____ - Overall grade determined by class atten, participation, musical theory comprehension, reports - _____ - _____ - _____
3. _____ - Violin, flute, clarinet $ - _____ - _____ - _____	3. _____ - Violins and flutes manufactured in great quantities - _____ - _____ - _____

Integrated Essay

The reading passage claims that mandatory music classes _____

_____.

However, the listening passage argues that _____

_____.

To begin with, the writer claims that _____

_____.

The majority of the students who graduate from college pursue careers in

science, business or technology. _____

_____.

_____.

_____.

On the other hand, the speaker contradicts this claim by stating that _____

_____.

Music classes actually stimulate other classes. _____

_____.

_____.

_____.

Furthermore, the author mentions that _____
_____.

Some students have absolutely no natural talent when it comes to music. _____
_____.
_____.
_____.

Conversely, the lecturer goes against this by stating that _____
_____.

A student's overall grade is determined by class attendance, participation, understanding of musical theory, and reports. _____
_____.
_____.
_____.

Moreover, the text argues that _____
_____.

Violins, flutes, and clarinets are very expensive. _____
_____.
_____.
_____.

On the contrary, the lecture challenges this argument by stating that _____
_____.

Violins and flutes are manufactured in mass quantities, so the prices are cheap.
_____.
_____.
_____.

Vocabulary:

mandatory	adj.	required by law or rules; compulsory.	*obligatory, required*
pursue	v.	seek to attain or accomplish (a goal) over a long period.	*strive, seek*
practical	adj.	of or concerned with the actual doing or use of something rather than with theory and ideas.	*applied, pragmatic*
assess	v.	evaluate or estimate the nature, ability, or quality of.	*evaluate, judge*
essential	adj.	absolutely necessary; extremely important.	*crucial, vital*
burden	n.	a duty or misfortune that causes hardship, anxiety, or grief; a nuisance.	*responsibility, onus*
stimulate	v.	encourage interest or activity in (a person or animal).	*encourage, prompt*
manufacture	v.	make (something) on a large scale using machinery.	*produce, construct*
bulk	n.	large in quantity or amount.	

Sample Essay

The reading passage claims that mandatory music classes will bring about a few problems. However, the listening passage argues that the problems mentioned in the reading are non-existent.

To begin with, the writer claims that music classes do not prepare students for a career in society. The majority of the students who graduate from college pursue careers in science, business or technology. The purpose of going to school is to learn information and gain experience which will help them later in life. Subjects like mathematics and science will provide valuable information to students, not music. On the other hand, the speaker contradicts this claim by stating that music classes actually stimulate other classes. Music classes teach rhythms and theories, which can be applied to math and science courses. Also, music classes help expand a student's imagination. This can help students when they write creative essays in literature class or make nontraditional projects. Therefore, music classes will influence other subjects and help students enter the university of their choice and get a good job.

Furthermore, the author mentions that assessing and giving grades in music classes are unfair. Some students have absolutely no natural talent when it comes to music. Years of practice may not result in perfection. Then these students will likely fail in their classes, which will prevent them from being accepted into a good university or even get a job. Conversely, the lecturer goes against this by stating that a student's grade is not determined by how well they can create music. A student's overall grade is determined by class attendance, participation, understanding of musical theory, and reports. So a student's hard work will help them get a passing grade and they will not be discouraged from taking the class.

Moreover, the text argues that musical instruments are expensive. Violins, flutes, and clarinets are very costly. Students who come from low income families will find it burdensome to purchase such an instrument. Maintenance and repair are expensive as well. On the contrary, the lecture challenges this argument by stating that there are many solutions to overcome this cost. Violins and flutes are manufactured in mass quantities, so the prices are cheap. Also, schools purchase instruments so that students can borrow them like library books. So instruments being costly should not prevent students from taking music classes.

388 words

Practice 4

Genetically modified organisms, or GMOs are organisms that have been genetically modified to better suit the needs of humans. Most GMOs are fruits, plants, and livestock humans eat in their daily sustenance. Proponents of GMO will argue that it is necessary for several reasons.

Without this genetically altered food sustenance, humans will face a shortage on food. GMOs have been made so that food can be grown in a short amount of time and be grown all year long without the restraint on weather or seasonal conditions. For example, tomatoes have been inserted with a specific gene found in arctic fish. Arctic fish swim in water temperature below freezing, so their body emits an antifreeze chemical that allows the fish to survive in such frigid conditions. This antifreeze gene was inserted into the DNA of a tomato so that tomatoes can be grown even during cold winter days. Such genetic modifications allow food to never fall short.

Furthermore, genetically altered organisms have been around for thousands of years. Although Gregor Mendel, the father of genetics, is credited with altering the gene pool for peas to produce wanted characteristics, humans have been creating GMOs since 8000 BCE. Farmers and herders used selective breeding and cross-breeding to create plants and animals with desirable traits. Since then, no hazardous side effects were noticed and people who consume GMOs have not shown any illnesses or unwanted side effects from them. So it is safe to say that GMOs are safe to eat and that consumers should not be wary of them.

Lastly, through the engineering process of creating GMOs, scientist have taken great strides in the field of genetics. By analyzing the DNA of organisms, scientists have come to understand the complexity of genetics and have learned to apply what they learned in areas outside of simple food. For instance, pharmaceutical companies have utilized specific traits of plants and animals in creating improved drugs that benefit mankind. As such, thanks to GMOs, science has advanced further in its path.

Reading Notetaking

Reading	Listening
Main: GMO's are _____	

1. _____
 	
   - GMO made so food grow fast and year-long
 	
     - _____
 	
     - _____
 	
     - _____	

2. _____
 	
   - Humans create GMOs since 8000 BCE
 	
     - _____
 	
     - _____
 	
     - _____	

3. _____
 	
   - Analyze DNA and apply to food
 	
     - _____
 	
     - _____
 	
     - _____	

(CH2-4.mp3)

Listening Notetaking

Reading	Listening
Main: GMO's are _____	**Main:** _____

1. _____
- GMO made so food grow fast and year-long
  - _____
  - _____
  - _____
	1. _____
	- _____
	- _____
	- _____
	- _____

2. _____
- Humans create GMOs since 8000 BCE
  - _____
  - _____
  - _____
	2. _____
	- _____
	- _____
	- _____

3. _____
- Analyze DNA and apply to food
  - _____
  - _____
  - _____
	3. _____
	- _____
	- _____
	- _____

Integrated Essay

The reading passage claims that genetically modified organisms (GMO) are _____
_____.

However, the listening passage argues that _____
_____.

To begin with, the writer claims that _____
_____.

GMOs are made so that food can be produced in a short amount of time and be available all year long. _____
_____.
_____.

On the other hand, the speaker contradicts this claim by stating that _____
_____.
_____.
_____.
_____.

Furthermore, the author mentions that _____
_____.

Humans have been making GMOs since 8000 BCE. _____
_____.
_____.
_____.

Conversely, the lecturer goes against this by stating that _____
_____.
_____.
_____.
_____.
_____.

Moreover, the text argues that _____
_____.

Scientists have analyzed the DNA of different organisms and have applied what they learned in producing simple GMO food. _____
_____.
_____.
_____.

On the contrary, the lecture challenges this argument by stating that _____
_____.
_____.
_____.
_____.

Vocabulary:

modified	v.	make partial or minor changes to (something), typically so as to improve it or to make it less extreme.	*alter, change*
sustenance	n.	food and drink regarded as a source of strength; nourishment.	*nourishment, food*
proponent	n.	a person who advocates a theory, proposal, or project.	*advocate, supporter*
alter	v.	change or cause to change in character or composition, typically in a comparatively small but significant way.	*change, adjust*
restraint	n.	a measure or condition that keeps someone or something under control or within limits.	*constraint, check*
emit	v.	produce and discharge (something, especially gas or radiation).	*release, discharge*
frigid	adj.	very cold in temperature.	*freezing, icy*
credit	n.	public acknowledgment or praise, typically that given or received when a person's responsibility for an action or idea becomes or is made apparent.	*commendation, praise*
hazardous	adj.	risky; dangerous.	*dangerous, risky*
wary	adj.	feeling or showing caution about possible dangers or problems.	*cautious, careful*
stride	n.	a step or stage in progress toward an aim.	*progress, advance*
advance	v.	move forward in a purposeful way.	*proceed, press on*
erroneous	adj.	wrong; incorrect.	*wrong, incorrect*
temporary	adj.	lasting for only a limited period of time; not permanent.	*short-term, interim*
contribute	v.	give (something, especially money) in order to help achieve or provide something.	*give, donate*
diagnose	v.	identify the nature of (an illness or other problem) by examination of the symptoms.	*identify, determine*
coincidence	n.	a remarkable concurrence of events or circumstances without apparent causal connection.	*chance, destiny*
dormant	adj.	temporarily inactive or inoperative.	*asleep, reposing*
meddle	v.	interfere in or busy oneself unduly with something that is not one's concern.	*interfere, intrude*
affair	n.	a matter that is a particular person's concern or responsibility.	*concern, matter*
realm	n.	a field or domain of activity or interest.	*domain, area*
taboo	n.	a social or religious custom prohibiting or forbidding discussion of a particular practice or forbidding association with a particular person, place, or thing.	*prohibition, ban*
appeal	v.	apply to a higher court for a reversal of (the decision of a lower court).	*implore, beseech*
ban	v.	officially or legally prohibit.	*forbid, veto*

Sample Essay

The reading passage claims that genetically modified organisms (GMOs) are necessary for several reasons. However, the listening passage argues that the points mentioned in the reading are erroneous.

To begin with, the writer claims that GMOs provide plenty of food to eat. GMOs are made so that food can be produced in a short amount of time and be available all year long. An example is a tomato with the antifreeze gene of an arctic fish, which prevents the tomato from freezing during winter. On the other hand, the speaker contradicts this claim by stating that GMOs are a temporary solution to food shortage because of the negative side effects of farming GMOs. To farm GMOs, certain pesticides must be used which will only temporarily wipe out its intended pest. But these pests will resurface and new pesticide resistant bugs will eat non-GMO produce and there will be nothing left for the farmers.

Furthermore, the author mentions that GMOs have been around for a long time. Humans have been making GMOs since 8000 BCE. Selective breeding and cross breeding are used to create plants and animals with specific traits. No hazardous side effects have been observed and people who eat GMOs have not shown any illnesses or undesirable side effects from them. Conversely, the lecturer goes against this by stating that it is wrong to assume that GMOs are safe to eat. Scientists believe that GMOs are related to various types of cancer. More cases of cancer have surfaced at around the same time GMOs were sold to consumers. Since cancer is found dormant in every human, it is believed that years of eating GMO products mutated human's DNA and more cancer patients have been diagnosed.

Moreover, the text argues that there have been great advancements in the field of genetics by creating GMOs. Scientists have analyzed the DNA of different organisms and have applied what they learned from producing simple GMO food. For example, pharmaceutical companies have used plants and animal traits to create medicinal drugs. On the contrary, the lecture challenges this argument by stating that people should not meddle with godly affairs. Many people believe that each organism was created by a superior being for a specific purpose. Religious groups call GMOs a taboo and hold rallies to ban GMOs from their country. They believe that advancements should come from hard work alone.

396 words

Practice 5

In recent years, the use of electronic voting booths to conduct votes have become more widespread. This method of gathering votes has several advantages.

The first advantage is that a wider number of people can have access to voting using this method. Votes are taken by a simple touch on the screen, so voters can go in and out of the booths in rapid succession. Since electronic voting booths are machines, it does not tire so it will not need any breaks throughout the day. Also, voting booths can be placed in different parts of the city. When voting is administered by humans, there were a limited number of locations where voters could go and cast their vote. However, since the electronic booths do not require human administration, they can be placed in local supermarkets or banks so that anyone can have access to it anytime.

The second advantage of electronic voting booths is that accurate votes can be cast. Some people have poor penmanship, so writing their votes has proven to be misleading at times. Also, electronic voting booths do not require human interaction. While waiting in line to vote or when confronted with the administrator, opinions can be exchanged, and the voter can be swayed to vote for the other side. Since voting booths are enclosed in a veil and the only interaction the voter gets is with a non-opinionated computer screen, they can make unbiased decisions.

A third advantage of electronic voting booth is that the chance of errors is lower. When counting votes, humans are prone to make mistakes while counting; however, machines have no margins of error since the votes are cast electronically. Sometimes, the questions or phrases in the paper ballots can be worded in a confusing manner, so that non-native English speakers or the elderly may have trouble understanding how or what to vote. However, computer screens are color coded and the options are displayed in a simple manner, so there is less chance to make a mistake.

Reading Notetaking

Reading	Listening
Main: _____	

1. _____
     - _____
     - _____
     - _____
     - _____	

2. _____
     - _____
     - _____
     - _____
     - _____	

3. _____
     - _____
     - _____
     - _____
     - _____	

(CH2-5.mp3)

Listening Notetaking

Reading	Listening
Main: _____	Main: _____
1. _____ - _____ - _____ - _____ - _____	1. _____ - _____ - _____ - _____ - _____
2. _____ - _____ - _____ - _____ - _____	2. _____ - _____ - _____ - _____ - _____
3. _____ - _____ - _____ - _____ - _____	3. _____ - _____ - _____ - _____ - _____

Integrated Essay

The reading passage claims that _____
_____.

However, the listening passage argues that _____
_____.

To begin with, the writer claims that _____
_____
_____
_____
_____.

On the other hand, the speaker contradicts this claim by stating that _____
_____
_____
_____
_____
_____
_____.

Furthermore, the author mentions that _____

_____.

_____.

_____.

_____.

Conversely, the lecturer goes against this by stating that _____

_____.

_____.

_____.

_____.

_____.

Moreover, the text argues that _____

_____.

_____.

_____.

_____.

On the contrary, the lecture challenges this argument by stating that _____

_____.

_____.

_____.

_____.

_____.

Vocabulary:

conduct	v.	organize and carry out.	*manage, direct*
succession	n.	a number of people or things sharing a specified characteristic and following one after the other.	*series, progression*
tire	v.	feel or cause to feel in need of rest or sleep.	*weaken*
administration	n.	the process or activity of running a business, organization, etc.	*management, command*
penmanship	n.	the art or skill of writing by hand.	
sway	v.	control or influence (a person or course of action).	*influence, affect*
veil	n.	a thing that serves to cover, conceal, or disguise.	*covering, screen*
unbiased	adj.	showing no prejudice for or against something; impartial.	*impartial, neutral*
prone	adj.	likely to or liable to suffer from, do, or experience something, typically something regrettable or unwelcome.	*inclined, susceptible*
margin	n.	an amount by which a thing is won or falls short.	*amount, difference*
misled	v.	cause (someone) to have a wrong idea or impression about someone or something.	*deceive, delude*
delay	v.	make (someone or something) late or slow.	*detain, retard*
deploy	v.	bring into effective action; utilize.	*use, employ*
flaw	n.	a mark, fault, or other imperfection that mars a substance or object.	*defect blemish*
strategically	adv.	in a way that relates to the achievement of long-term or overall aims and interests.	
elude	v.	evade or escape from (a danger, enemy, or pursuer), typically in a skillful or cunning way.	*evade, avoid*
hesitant	adj.	tentative, unsure, or slow in acting or speaking.	*uncertain, doubtful*
clever	adj.	quick to understand, learn, and devise or apply ideas; intelligent.	*bright, talented*
mediator	n.	a person who attempts to make people involved in a conflict come to an agreement; a go-between.	*negotiator, middleman*
verdict	n.	a decision on a disputed issue in a civil or criminal case or an inquest.	*judgement, decision*

Sample Essay

The reading passage claims that electronic voting booths have several advantages. However, the listening passage argues that this type of voting method has some serious problems.

To begin with, the writer claims that more people can have access to voting with the electronic voting booths. Since the votes are cast by a simple touch on a screen, there will be a rapid succession of voters. The voting machines can also be placed in different parts of the city, such as local supermarkets or banks, so that anyone can vote anytime. On the other hand, the speaker contradicts this claim by stating that voting machines are likely to break down and halt the voting process. Then people will be delayed from voting and not even have a chance to vote. In the recent presidential election, a few of the machines made by the same company had released their voting booths with a mechanical flaw. When these machines did not function on the day of the vote, thousands of people failed to participate in the election process.

Furthermore, the author mentions that when using electronic voting booths, accurate votes can be cast. Some people have poor penmanship, so it can be misleading. Also, because there is no human presence, voters can make unbiased decisions. Conversely, the lecturer goes against this by stating that electronic voting booths do not give accurate votes. Even though there are no humans present, the machines are placed around different candidate's territory. So banners, rallies, and chants will still cause the voter to be swayed. It is similar to a soccer fan trying to cheer for his home team while being mixed in with the opponent's crowd.

Moreover, the text argues that the chance of error is lower with a machine. Machines have no margins of error since the counting is done electronically. Moreover, screens are color coded and the options are shown in a simple manner, so there is little room for mistakes. On the contrary, the lecture challenges this argument by stating that electronic voting booths can still make errors in counting since they can be hacked. As long as they are connected to a network, all machines have the probability of being compromised. With a few algorithms, a clever hacker can change the number of votes to the winning side. Therefore, important votes are written on paper and given to the mediator to be counted, while a second mediator confirms the count amongst developed countries around the world. Even a jury passes judgement on a victim by utilizing paper votes to give to the judge.

430 words

Chapter notes:

CHAPTER 03

Academic Discussion Lesson

Academic Discussion Essay

The objective of an academic discussion is to state and support your opinion about a given topic in an online class discussion. A good response should contain appropriate reasons, examples, and details to support your point of view.

Academic discussion question type:

> Your professor is teaching a class on *subject.* Write a post responding to the professor's question.
>
> **In your response you should:**
> - Express and support your opinion
> - Make a contribution to the discussion
>
> An effective response will contain at least 100 words.
> You will have 10 minutes to write it.
>
> **Professor**
> Online class discussion, professor's question.
> **Student A**
> Student's opinion
> **Student B**
> Student's opinion

The test taker is given 10 minutes to write the academic discussion essay. As soon as the question is given, it is important to brainstorm and outline so that an organized and logical essay can be produced.

Sample question:

Your professor is teaching a class on sociology.
Write a post responding to the professor's question.

In your response you should:
- Express and support your opinion
- Make a contribution to the discussion

An effective response will contain at least 100 words.
You will have 10 minutes to write it.

Dr. Jones
When a person commits a crime, they are punished according to the severity of the act. Still, the majority of criminals are sent to prison for a set length of time. As the number of people being sent to prison is increasing annually, some people believe that this is the best way to solve crime. Others think that community service is better. If you were to choose one punishment, which would you say is the best method? Why?

Michelle
It is obvious for a person to be responsible for their crime by serving time in prison. While spending time in confinement, individuals will have time to reflect upon their mistakes and think of ways to become a better citizen. Still, some criminals will refuse to change and will pose a threat to society. So it would be best to lock them up so that they can never commit the same heinous act again.

David
I disagree with Michelle that the best way to punish criminals is sending them to prison. Community service is actually the best way to punish law breakers. Since criminals carried out their crimes in self-interest, it is best that they serve the community for their crimes. Therefore, I think criminals should be punished by giving them community service.

Subjective or objective?

It is important to note that although an academic discussion is asking for the test taker's opinion, it is actually beneficial to write an objective essay, rather than one that is subjective.

Brainstorming and outlining:

As mentioned beforehand, in order to write an objective essay, your reasons are more important than your preference or opinion. Test takers should spend about a minute brainstorming their ideas before typing their essay. Here are just some of the most common reasons test takers can use in their essays.

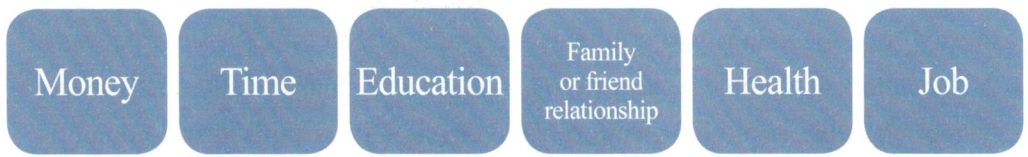

Additional note:

As you can see, there are more reasons to punish criminals by sending them to prison. Also, notice that you can choose the reasons stated by the other students. You could choose to write your essay with the reasons they gave or support your preference with new reasons. But make sure to add your own opinion to the discussion and not just rewrite ideas that have already been stated. What is important is how much logic and explanation you can write in your essay.

For example, you might agree with Michelle that prison time will allow individuals to reflect upon their past mistakes. However, you will need to add your own ideas for this point of view. For instance, you could argue that individuals can meditate and write journals. This will help them to organize their thoughts and even bring it up during therapy sessions they have in prison. This would become additional support for Michelle's point of view while introducing your ideas.

Academic discussion rubric:

Score	Description
5	**A completely successful response** The essay is coherent and clearly contributes to the online discussion. It also shows consistent demonstration in the use of the English language. A typical essay of this score shows the following: • Coherent and logical explanations, examples, and/or details • Proper use of sentence structures and vocabulary • Almost no vocabulary or grammatical errors
4	**A generally successful response** The essay is coherent to the online discussion and the language used allows the writer's ideas to be understood. A typical essay of this score shows the following: • Coherent and adequate explanations, examples, and/or details • A variation of sentence structures and vocabulary • Minimal vocabulary or grammatical errors
3	**A partially successful response** The essay is mostly coherent and mostly contributes to the online discussion. It also shows some understanding of the English language. A typical essay of this score shows the following: • Some parts of the explanations, examples, and/or details are missing or unclear • Some variety in sentence structures and vocabulary • Noticeable mistakes in vocabulary and grammar
2	**A mostly unsuccessful response** The essay shows an attempt to contribute to the online discussion, but is limited in the use of the English language and makes it hard to understand. A typical essay of this score shows the following: • Ideas that are poorly explained or partially relevant • A limited range of sentence structures and vocabulary • Major mistakes in vocabulary and grammar
1	**An unsuccessful response** The essay is ineffective in attempting to contribute to the online discussion. The use of the English language is very limited and prevents any ideas to be expressed. A typical essay of this score shows the following: • Few or no coherent ideas • Severe limitation on sentence structure variety, as well as vocabulary • Constant errors in the use of the English language

Academic Discussion Organization:

Introduction
- Introduce the topic or provide background information
- Your opinion or preference

Explanation 1
- Explanation to your opinion or preference
- Example
- Counterexample (when applicable)

Explanation 2
- Explanation to your opinion or preference
- Example
- Counterexample (when applicable)

Conclusion
- Restate your opinion or preference

Introduction:

The introductory sentence introduces the topic and the opinion of the writer. Attention grabbers are used to start the introduction with a general statement. Test takers may write an interesting fact, cite recent news, use a famous quote, or state something obvious.

(Interesting fact)

There are more than ten million people serving time in prison throughout the world. Approximately twenty percent of those incarcerated are in the United States.

(Famous quote)

Albert Einstein once said, "Only a life lived for others is a life worthwhile." This shows how a person's life is fulfilled by serving the community.

(Topic of discussion)

The professor argues about the appropriate punishment for those who have committed acts of crime.

The last sentence in the introductory portion of the essay has to mention the writer's opinion or preference to the professor's question.

Good: *In regards to giving an appropriate punishment, sending criminals to prison is the better solution.*

Sometimes, writers may choose to mention a new solution altogether. Remember, the professor specifically asked to choose between prison or community service. Writers should only choose from the choices the professor writes in the discussion. Do not get confused with writing new reasons outside the ones mentioned by the students.

Bad: *I believe that criminals should be punished by monetary means; they should pay an appropriate amount for the crimes they committed.*

Your introductory sentences should not be long. It should not introduce any specific ideas and should not take no more than 2 minutes writing it.

Body:

This is the most important part in the academic discussion. This is where logic and explanation steps in to support your opinion or preference.

Explanation:	Write two or three sentences that support your reason or preference.
Example:	Talk about a personal experience, news, history, historical figure, or statistics to support your explanation.
Counterexample:	An example or a statement that shows the weakness of the opposite opinion or option compared to your opinion or preference.

Explanation:	*Spending time in prison will allow individuals to reflect upon their past mistakes. Just as children are given a time out to think about what they did wrong when they misbehave, criminals should be given a time out in prison. During their time in prison, felons will be able to think back on their crimes and perhaps atone for their crimes.*
Example:	*Nowadays, inmates are given journals to record their thoughts. Then, they share their thoughts with others in therapy or group counseling.*
Counterexample:	*However, criminals will not have a chance to repent for their crimes when they are doing community service since they will be too busy picking up trash or doing some sort of manual labor.*

One thing to note while writing the explanation is something called coherency. Coherency refers to the flow of ideas presented in the essay. Sentences must be connected to one another by sharing the same idea and explanation.

Bad coherency: *Spending time in prison will allow individuals to reflect upon their past mistakes. Community service does not allow for mediation since the body will be busy doing manual labor.*

The coherency in this paragraph is actually bad because the explanation starts off by stating that spending time in prison will allow individuals to reflect upon their past mistakes. So the next sentence should discuss why or how individuals are able to meditate in prison, but instead, it mentions why community service does not allow for reflection. Although this flow of idea may not sound wrong to the average person, sentences must be connected with what was written before.

Good coherency: *Spending time in prison will allow individuals to reflect upon their past mistakes. Just as children are given a time out to think about what they did wrong when they misbehave, criminals should be given a time out in prison.*

As you can see, the sentences are all connected because they discuss why criminals need to go to prison to think about what they did wrong.

Even the examples should be coherent with the sentences written before it.

Bad coherency: *During their time in prison, felons will be able to think back on their crimes and perhaps atone for their crimes. While wearing orange jumpsuits and picking trash along highways, criminals will have to focus on pick up trash and not getting hit by the incoming traffic.*

The example is not relevant to the explanation and does not discuss about felons being able to think back on their crimes while in prison. Here the example is not coherent to the explanation.

Good coherency: *During their time in prison, felons will be able to think back on their crimes and perhaps atone for their crimes. Nowadays, inmates are given journals to record their thoughts. Then, they share their thoughts with others in therapy or group counseling.*

The example and the explanation before it is connected by the same idea, which is felons being able to repent for their crimes in prison.

Conclusion:

This is the last sentence of the academic discussion essay. No new information should be stated here, only a restatement of the writer's opinion or preference.

> *Therefore, when it comes to passing the right punishment for criminals, sending them to prison is the better solution than having them do community service.*

Some test takers may not have enough time writing the concluding sentence. It may feel a bit awkward finishing the essay without a conclusion, especially if the last sentence is an example. The rubric does not state that a concluding sentence is necessary, but if test takers have the time to write one, they should definitely include one.

Edit:

Your essay is not complete until you have proofread your essay at least once. Believe it or not, even the best writers are prone to make mistakes when there is a set time to write the essay because they are in a rush to finish the essay before time runs out.

Simple mistakes include:
- Spelling errors
- Grammatical errors: subject verb agreement and pronoun agreement
- Capitalization errors
- Punctuation errors

These are mistakes which are simple to identify and should be corrected in the last minute or seconds from the 10 minutes given to write this essay.

Sample essay 1:

There are more than ten million people serving time in prison throughout the world. Approximately twenty percent of those incarcerated are in the United States. In regards to giving an appropriate punishment, sending criminals to prison is the better solution. Spending time in prison will allow individuals to reflect upon their past mistakes. Just as children are given a time out to think about what they did wrong when they misbehave, criminals should be given a time out in prison. During their time in prison, felons will be able to think back on their crimes and perhaps atone for their crimes. Nowadays, inmates are given journals to record their thoughts. Then, they share their thoughts with others in therapy or group counseling. However, criminals will not have a chance to repent for their crimes when they are doing community service since they will be too busy picking up trash or doing some sort of manual labor. Therefore, when it comes to passing the right punishment for criminals, sending them to prison is the better solution than having them do community service.

181 words.

Score: 5

This essay is a completely successful response. The writer chooses prison time as the best method for punishing criminals. The writer then provides an explanation of how prison time will allow felons to contemplate upon their crimes and repent for what they have done. The writer continues on to point out that community service lacks this meditation time, so it is not appropriate as a punishment. Overall, this essay provides coherent explanations and details to support the writer's preference and provides a relevant contribution to the professor's online discussion. The writer also uses some complex sentence structures and appropriate vocabulary.

Sample essay 2:

Criminals should pick up trash and do other community service as punishment for their crimes. These people were very selfish and committed crimes for their own benefit. For example, they may have robbed a bank to become rich. Or they may have stolen a car since they don't have one. Since criminals acted on their own self-interest, their punishment should be to serve others. By doing community service, like picking up trash, they will learn the importance of serving others and not be selfish. Thus, the best method to punish criminals is community service instead of sending them to prison.

100 words.

Score: 3

This essay is a partially successful response. The writer chooses community service as the best method for punishing criminals. The writer then provides an explanation of why community service is a fair punishment for criminals. However, it fails to explain more thoroughly why serving others is a fit punishment. The writer could have mentioned how going to prison will not be an act of serving others, so it is not a proper punishment for these selfish individuals. There is some variety in sentence structures, but the usage of vocabulary is limited. For example, the writer only uses the word "criminal" to describe those who committed crimes. Also the word count is exactly 100 words, which is the minimum word count for an academic discussion essay.

For the academic discussion essay, the official word count is 100 words. Similar to the integrated word count, the official word count is minimal and will not be enough to write a logical essay. A 200-word essay is adequate, but keep in mind that with more words, more mistakes can be made as well.

Why do you get a low score on the academic discussion essay?

1) Misunderstanding the essay question:
   Sometimes, test takers may rush reading the question and misinterpret it. Read the question carefully and make sure to answer the question completely. A simple word like "NOT" in the question can completely result in a different essay.

2) No logic:
   An academic discussion essay should not be a storybook; in other words, the example should not take up the entire essay. Logical explanation should be supported by an example, which should only be a few sentences.

3) Content:
   Most of the points will be deducted from this area. The explanations for your opinion must make sense, the coherency of the ideas written in the essay should match, and the organization of the essay should be clear.

4) Grammar and spelling mistakes:
   Yes, points will be deducted for making grammar and spelling mistakes. So make sure to edit the essay in the last minute.

5) Incomplete essay:
   The academic discussion only gives ten minutes to write. Be sure to check the time every now and then to finish writing the essay.

Chapter notes:

CHAPTER 04
Academic Discussion Practices

Practice 1

Your professor is teaching a class on environmental science.
Write a post responding to the professor's question.

In your response you should:
- Express and support your opinion
- Make a contribution to the discussion

An effective response will contain at least 100 words.
You will have 10 minutes to write it.

Professor Miller
With global warming threatening civilizations around the world, it has become essential to counteract the problems associated with the continuous increase in our planet's temperature. Scientists and environmentalists have proposed multiple solutions to help combat global warming. What would you consider as the most effective way to decrease global warming? Why?

Sarah
I would say that decreasing the use of gasoline cars will help alleviate the problems associated with global warming. Temperatures are increasing due to carbon emissions from gasoline powered cars and buses. If people use alternative transports, such as electric cars, then carbon emissions will decrease, and global warming will follow as well.

Jake
I think schools can do a better job educating students regarding the causes and effects of global warming. Most of my friends are actually unaware of what causes global warming and the dangers associated with it. If professors pass on information about global warming to their students, then the younger generation will be able to make changes in their lifestyle, which would ultimately affect global temperatures in the future.

Brainstorm and Organization

Introduction	
Explanation 1	
Explanation 2	
Conclusion	

Essay

Your professor is teaching a class on environmental science.
Write a post responding to the professor's question.

In your response you should:
- Express and support your opinion
- Make a contribution to the discussion

An effective response will contain at least 100 words.
You will have 10 minutes to write it.

Professor Miller
With global warming threatening civilizations around the world, it has become essential to counteract the problems associated with the continuous increase in our planet's temperature. Scientists and environmentalists have proposed multiple solutions to help combat global warming. What would you consider as the most effective way to decrease global warming? Why?

Sarah
I would say that decreasing the use of gasoline cars will help alleviate the problems associated with global warming. Temperatures are increasing due to carbon emissions from gasoline powered cars and buses. If people use alternative transports, such as electric cars, then carbon emissions will decrease, and global warming will follow as well.

Jake
I think schools can do a better job educating students regarding the causes and effects of global warming. Most of my friends are actually unaware of what causes global warming and the dangers associated with it. If professors pass on information about global warming to their students, then the younger generation will be able to make changes in their lifestyle, which would ultimately affect global temperatures in the future.

Sample Essay 1

There are many different methods to fight global warming. In my opinion, I believe the best way to solve global warming is to use environmental friendly cars. I agree with Sarah that carbon emissions is one of the root causes of global warming. I would like to add that using alternative fuels like hydrogen fuel produces zero carbon emissions and therefore not contribute to global warming. Jake offered the solution of educating students, but this is not an effective solution. I was taught about global warming when I was in elementary school, but to be honest, I was too young to care about the dangers of global warming. I was too busy trying to play with my friends. Therefore, the best way to solve global warming is to use non-gasoline cars.

131 words

Sample Essay 2

There is actually a hole in the ozone layer, which permits harmful sunlight to enter the atmosphere. This is one of the causes of global warming. The most practical solution to decrease global warming is to stop using products that use HCFCs or CFCs as propellants. These chemicals are responsible for weakening the ozone layer. By halting the use of products that use these chemicals, the ozone layer will be restored. Some of the products that use HCFCs or CFCs include air conditioning units, refrigerators, and hair sprays. People can use household appliances that use safer chemicals and style their hair with water based hair sprays. Then, global warming will surely come to a stop.

115 words

Chapter notes:

Practice 2

Your professor is teaching a class on social studies.
Write a post responding to the professor's question.

In your response you should:
- Express and support your opinion
- Make a contribution to the discussion

An effective response will contain at least 100 words.
You will have 10 minutes to write it.

Dr. Johnson
I'd like to discuss the impact of social media on society. The initial stages of social media started with simple postings of text messages. Then suddenly, people were able to upload pictures and videos to show the world what they were up to. Of course, such advancement is prone to have pros and cons. On one side, people applaud social media for connecting people around the world. On the other side, critics claim that social media spreads false information and gives rise to cyberbullying. What is your stand on social media? Is it a beneficial tool, or something that causes harm?

Andrea
Social media is a benefit to society, without a doubt. With social media platforms like Facebook and Instagram, I was able to connect with old friends whom I have not seen for many years. Social media also helps people to stay connected when they are distant from one another. I have a cousin in South Korea, whom I am able to stay in touch with here in the United States because of social media platforms.

William
Social media does more harm than good. So many people are addicted to social media platforms that they spend more than half a day looking at random people's profiles or posting pictures of themselves every second. Instead of socializing with family and friends in front of them, people are too busy looking at their online friends and seeing what they are up to.

Brainstorming and Organization

Introduction	
Explanation 1	
Explanation 2	
Conclusion	

Essay

Your professor is teaching a class on social studies.
Write a post responding to the professor's question.

In your response you should:
- Express and support your opinion
- Make a contribution to the discussion

An effective response will contain at least 100 words.
You will have 10 minutes to write it.

Dr. Johnson
I'd like to discuss the impact of social media on society. The initial stages of social media started with simple postings of text messages. Then suddenly, people were able to upload pictures and videos to show the world what they were up to. Of course, such advancement is prone to have pros and cons. On one side, people applaud social media for connecting people around the world. On the other side, critics claim that social media spreads false information and gives rise to cyberbullying. What is your stand on social media? Is it a beneficial tool, or something that causes harm?

Andrea
Social media is a benefit to society, without a doubt. With social media platforms like Facebook and Instagram, I was able to connect with old friends whom I have not seen for many years. Social media also helps people to stay connected when they are distant from one another. I have a cousin in South Korea, whom I am able to stay in touch with here in the United States because of social media platforms.

William
Social media does more harm than good. So many people are addicted to social media platforms that they spend more than half a day looking at random people's profiles or posting pictures of themselves every second. Instead of socializing with family and friends in front of them, people are too busy looking at their online friends and seeing what they are up to.

Sample Essay 1

The professor discusses whether social media is beneficial or harmful to society. I believe that social media does more harm than good. I agree with William that people spend way too much time on social media. Instead of spending quality time with the people directly in front of them, social media users would rather spend their time on their smartphones or computers. Because of this, the significance of genuine relationships have been deteriorating in our society. Whenever I walk into a coffee shop, I would see couples and friends staring into their phones and looking at social media platforms instead of talking with the person in front of them. This has broken up families and friends since the biggest importance in any relationship is having a conversation. Instead, social media prohibited conversations from occurring and glued people's eyes onto digital screens. Thus, social media harms society by taking away genuine relationships.

151 words

Sample Essay 2

Facebook recently installed a video chat system onto their platform. So now, users can see the faces of their loved ones. Like this, social media is an essential part of society and people should embrace the advantages that it offers. To start off, social media allows people to post status or pictures of themselves so that others can know how they are doing. In South Korea, there is a saying, "No news is good news." So even though your family or friends may not call you, just seeing their status or pictures on social media will let you know that they are doing well. Furthermore, social media allows new relationships to be formed. Often times, people are too busy studying or working that they have no time to go out and make the effort to make new friends. However, social media connects people based on their hobbies and interests, so that users will not have to put in so much effort in making new friends. Therefore, social media is beneficial in our society.

173 words

Chapter notes:

Practice 3

Your professor is teaching a class on education.
Write a post responding to the professor's question.

In your response you should:
- Express and support your opinion
- Make a contribution to the discussion

An effective response will contain at least 100 words.
You will have 10 minutes to write it.

Professor Kimberly
Today in class, I would like to talk about the best method for grading students. Now, the majority of you are given grades based on the tests that you take periodically. Of course, there are alternatives to giving out examinations. Some of my colleagues grade their students based on their participation in class. Others give grades based on the homework that they turn in. Still, some mark their students solely on class attendance. There are many other methods to grading students. Which method of grading do you think is the most effective way? Why?

Mark
I believe that the best way to grade students is on homework. Some students, like myself, have a hard time memorizing chunks of information to prepare for a test. However, a homework assignment checks to make sure that students understood the lesson that was delivered that week. I believe that as long as students understand the concept that was taught that week, grading based on homework should be sufficient.

Jessica
The best method for grading students is the one most professors utilize; giving out examinations. A midterm exam or a final exam is a great way to make sure that students have a comprehensive understanding of the class. Anyone can remember the day's lesson, but not everyone can remember and understand several weeks' worth of information. Thus, having students take tests is a sure way to mark their intelligence.

Brainstorming and Organization

Introduction	
Explanation 1	
Explanation 2	
Conclusion	

Essay

Your professor is teaching a class on education.
Write a post responding to the professor's question.

In your response you should:
- Express and support your opinion
- Make a contribution to the discussion

An effective response will contain at least 100 words.
You will have 10 minutes to write it.

Professor Kimberly
Today in class, I would like to talk about the best method for grading students. Now, the majority of you are given grades based on the tests that you take periodically. Of course, there are alternatives to giving out examinations. Some of my colleagues grade their students based on their participation in class. Others give grades based on the homework that they turn in. Still, some mark their students solely on class attendance. There are many other methods to grading students. Which method of grading do you think is the most effective way? Why?

Mark
I believe that the best way to grade students is on homework. Some students, like myself, have a hard time memorizing chunks of information to prepare for a test. However, a homework assignment checks to make sure that students understood the lesson that was delivered that week. I believe that as long as students understand the concept that was taught that week, grading based on homework should be sufficient.

Jessica
The best method for grading students is the one most professors utilize; giving out examinations. A midterm exam or a final exam is a great way to make sure that students have a comprehensive understanding of the class. Anyone can remember the day's lesson, but not everyone can remember and understand several weeks' worth of information. Thus, having students take tests is a sure way to mark their intelligence.

Sample Essay 1

The goal of education is for students to learn. If students are burdened by grades, they will lose the opportunity to learn valuable lessons. In order to decrease this burden, the most effective way to grade students is grading based on participation. While participating, students are displaying their understanding to the professor, at the same time showing their curiosity towards the lesson. After all, being curious in a subject is the first step in acquiring knowledge. So when students are graded based on their participation, not only will they have less stress, but they will have an open mind to be curious. Other methods of grading will inhibit students from participating and showing an inquisitive mind, so those methods should be prohibited from grading students.

125 words

Sample Essay 2

The professor mentions several methods for grading students; however, I believe that the best way to grade a student is through tests and examinations. I agree with Jessica in that examinations are a great way to check a student's comprehensive understanding of the class. I would also like to point out that grades based on tests are reflective of what students will be judged on in their future careers. For example, when working in a corporate office, employees will be evaluated based on the works that they produce. These works will be comprehensive assignments, based on their work experience and knowledge they accumulated. Mark's opinion that homework is the best way to grade a student falls short of finding out their comprehensive understanding of the subject. Therefore, in order to prepare students for their future careers and how they will be assessed, grading them based on examinations is the most effective way.

152 words

Chapter notes:

Practice 4

Your professor is teaching a class on political science.
Write a post responding to the professor's question.

In your response you should:
- Express and support your opinion
- Make a contribution to the discussion

An effective response will contain at least 100 words.
You will have 10 minutes to write it.

Dr. Morales
Let's discuss whether the government should implement higher tax on unhealthy products, like cigarette and alcohol. By mandating a higher tax on these products, people will be discouraged from consuming them and reduce any health problems associated with the products. Still, some people argue that enforcing such high taxes is unfair since it takes away certain pleasures citizens receive from taking these products. What do you think? Why?

Maria
The government has no right to enforce higher taxes on goods like cigarette and alcohol. I understand that the government wants to help people not to indulge on these products so that they can live in good shape, but it is not the role of a country to force its citizens to live a healthy lifestyle. What people do to their bodies should be for the people to decide.

Richard
Since a government exists for the welfare of the people, they have every right to implement higher taxes on products that are not good for the body. A government is like a mother. If the mother sees her children consuming harmful products into their bodies, she should stop them at all costs. By enforcing higher taxes, the people will be burdened by the extra cost, so they will stop purchasing these harmful products.

Brainstorming and Organization

Introduction	_____ _____ _____
Explanation 1	_____ _____ _____ _____ _____
Explanation 2	_____ _____ _____ _____ _____
Conclusion	_____ _____ _____

Essay

Your professor is teaching a class on political science.
Write a post responding to the professor's question.

In your response you should:
- Express and support your opinion
- Make a contribution to the discussion

An effective response will contain at least 100 words.
You will have 10 minutes to write it.

Dr. Morales
Let's discuss whether the government should implement higher tax on unhealthy products, like cigarette and alcohol. By mandating a higher tax on these products, people will be discouraged from consuming them and reduce any health problems associated with the products. Still, some people argue that enforcing such high taxes is unfair since it takes away certain pleasures citizens receive from taking these products. What do you think? Why?

Maria
The government has no right to enforce higher taxes on goods like cigarette and alcohol. I understand that the government wants to help people not to indulge on these products so that they can live in good shape, but it is not the role of a country to force its citizens to live a healthy lifestyle. What people do to their bodies should be for the people to decide.

Richard
Since a government exists for the welfare of the people, they have every right to implement higher taxes on products that are not good for the body. A government is like a mother. If the mother sees her children consuming harmful products into their bodies, she should stop them at all costs. By enforcing higher taxes, the people will be burdened by the extra cost, so they will stop purchasing these harmful products.

Sample Essay 1

Taxes are paid by citizens to support the country they live in. From these taxes, the government uses the money to improve the welfare of the people. If increased taxes on cigarettes and alcohol will help maintain the health of the citizens, then it is permissible for the government to mandate such taxes. Like Richard said, the government is like a mother and should monitor the citizens so that they live healthy lives. Furthermore, governments would end up spending more money if its people find themselves in poor health due to cigarettes and alcohol. The country would have to build more medical facilities like hospitals to take in more patients, and the construction and maintenance of such facilities would require more tax money from the citizens. Therefore, in order to prevent sickness and disease while making sure no additional tax is paid to create additional infrastructures, the government should raise the tax on unhealthy products.

155 words

Sample Essay 2

There is a famous saying, "For the people, by the people." This simply states that the people should decide what's good for them. The government may try to interfere with the lifestyle of its citizens, but they have no right to tell them what to do. Thus, an increased tax on unhealthy products is a violation of the people's freedom and rights. I agree with Maria that the people should decide what they can do to their bodies. I would like to add that whatever consequence that comes from their decision should also be their responsibility. If individuals decide to harm their bodies by drinking alcohol and smoking, so be it. They are living like there is no tomorrow and enjoying life. However, it is also important to note that these individuals should not blame the government for lack of healthcare or rehabilitation programs. After all, it was their freedom and they decided to consume such unhealthy products. So people should be given the freedom to do whatever they wish to their bodies, and the government is wrong by implementing higher taxes in order to control their behavior.

188 words

Chapter notes:

Practice 5

Your professor is teaching a class on technology.
Write a post responding to the professor's question.

In your response you should:
- Express and support your opinion
- Make a contribution to the discussion

An effective response will contain at least 100 words.
You will have 10 minutes to write it.

Dr. Brown
Technology has advanced so much just in the past few decades. The creation of the Internet provided people with an abundance of information. The construction of efficient cars running on electricity has taken a step in solving air pollution. The latest craze is on metaverse and how it will change human interaction with people all around the world. Among the plethora of technological achievements, which do you think has had the most impact? Why?

Marty
I would say hovercrafts have made the most impact. Although it is not perfect yet, the creation of hovercraft has allowed people to traverse water and land without having to change vehicles. Also, the use of hovercrafts have proven to be effective in going over land mines that were planted in previous wars. Just in South Korea, where the 38th parallel line divides North and South Korea, hovercrafts have been used to disarm dangerous mines planted in the fields.

Jennifer
Social media platforms definitely has to be the most significant technological achievement. Platforms like Youtube, Facebook, and Instagram connected people from every corner of the world. Not only is information exchanged, but new relationships are able to be formed with people who share the same interest or hobby as you.

Brainstorming and Organization

Introduction	
Explanation 1	
Explanation 2	
Conclusion	

Essay

Your professor is teaching a class on technology.
Write a post responding to the professor's question.

In your response you should:
- Express and support your opinion
- Make a contribution to the discussion

An effective response will contain at least 100 words.
You will have 10 minutes to write it.

Dr. Brown
Technology has advanced so much just in the past few decades. The creation of the Internet provided people with an abundance of information. The construction of efficient cars running on electricity has taken a step in solving air pollution. The latest craze is on metaverse and how it will change human interaction with people all around the world. Among the plethora of technological achievements, which do you think has had the most impact? Why?

Marty
I would say hovercrafts have made the most impact. Although it is not perfect yet, the creation of hovercraft has allowed people to traverse water and land without having to change vehicles. Also, the use of hovercrafts have proven to be effective in going over land mines that were planted in previous wars. Just in South Korea, where the 38th parallel line divides North and South Korea, hovercrafts have been used to disarm dangerous mines planted in the fields.

Jennifer
Social media platforms definitely has to be the most significant technological achievement. Platforms like Youtube, Facebook, and Instagram connected people from every corner of the world. Not only is information exchanged, but new relationships are able to be formed with people who share the same interest or hobby as you.

Sample Essay 1

Ancient human civilizations were able to thrive due to the exchange of information between different cultures. This factor is still crucial in the modern world. So I believe that the invention of the Internet is the greatest technological achievement. Jennifer mentions social media platforms as the greatest invention; however, the Internet is the basis behind social media platforms. Without the Internet, users would not be able to upload their pictures or status online. Marty said that hovercrafts have had the greatest impact. But where did people get the information to build such a unique vehicle? Of course, it was from the Internet. It is clear that the Internet provided the groundwork for all other technological advancements, so it is without a doubt that the World Wide Web has had the greatest impact.

132 words

Sample Essay 2

The professor lists several important technological achievements. Still, I believe the technology that has made the most impact is vaccines. Up until the 19th century, people were unaware of what vaccines were and dreaded when they came down with a sickness or a disease, hoping that the ailment would not take their lives. However, with the creation of vaccines, people were given hope of overcoming whatever would attack them. For example, when the Covid19 virus first started to take the lives of its victims, the inflicted were scared of an imminent death. But within a year, a vaccine was made and many lives were saved. This Covid19 vaccine saved millions of lives all over the world. No other technological advancement was used by so many people. Thus, vaccines should be considered as the greatest technological stride.

136words

Actual Test
01

Writing Section Directions

Make sure that the headset is turned on.

This section will measure your ability to use writing as a form of communication in an academic setting. There are two writing tasks.

For the first writing task, you will be reading a passage and listening to a lecture. Then you will answer a question based on what you read and listened to. For the second writing task, you will write an academic discussion essay answering a question posed by the professor, using your experience and knowledge.

Now listen to the directions for the first writing task.

Writing Based on Reading and Listening

For this part, you will have **3 minutes** to read an academic passage. Afterwards, the passage will disappear and you will listen to a lecture regarding the same topic. You are recommended to take notes on both the reading and the listening.

Afterwards, you will have **20 minutes** to write an essay summarizing the relationship between the reading passage and the lecture. Try to summarize as completely as possible using information from the reading passage and the lecture. This section of the writing does not ask you to write your personal opinion. You will see the reading passage again when it is time to write. You may use the notes you took to help write the essay.

A good essay will be 150 to 225 words long. Your response will be assessed on the quality of your writing and on the accuracy and completeness of the content from the reading and the lecture. If you finish your essay before the time is over, you may click **NEXT** to go to the next writing section.

Now, the reading passage will appear for 3 minutes. Remember, the reading passage will be available to you again when you are writing. When the 3 minutes is over, the lecture will begin right away, so keep your headset on until the lecture is finished.

Reading

Question 1 of 2

00:03:00

As human population grows and cities expand, animals suffer from loss of habitats since their homes are destroyed by the construction of roads and buildings. A solution to rescue these animals have been proposed, which is to relocate the animals to a safe environment. However, there is mounting evidence that this method is not a practical solution.

To begin with, moving the animals to a new location can result in overpopulation. The new environment is already a home to a number of species with a balanced ecosystem and food scheme. With rescued animals moving in, there is bound to be overpopulation problems and animals will compete with one another for resource. This competition will lead to the demise of the animals since there will not be enough food, water, and living space. Therefore, the relocation solution may end up backfiring as the animals overcrowd and eventually starve to death from extreme competition.

Furthermore, relocating the animals may end up spreading unwanted disease to the new environment. Animals are carriers of many different diseases, so when they are moved to a new location, they unknowingly transport the diseases as well. This is a big problem because the animals in the new environment have never been exposed to the disease so they have little to no immunity. For example, there has been reported cases where endangered animals that were transported to the San Diego Zoo from mainland China carried mutated bird flu disease, so many of the animals in the zoo became sick.

Finally, there is a chance that animals may get injured and killed during the process of their capture. In order to move to a different location, animals must be captured first. Tranquilizer darts are used on the more massive and ferocious beasts, but at times, the dosage on the tranquilizers can be too much, which can lead to cardiac arrests on the animals that have been shot by it. Also, traps that have been set up to capture the animals may not provide adequate space and water once the animal is captured. When the trap captures the animal, sometimes it takes days for humans to retrieve it, but by the time they arrive, the animals have become dehydrated or suffered physical damage from confined space.

Listening

Question 1 of 2

(AT1.mp3)

Question 1 of 2

00:20:00

Directions: You have 20 minutes to organize and write your essay. Your essay will be assessed on the quality of your writing and how well you can summarize the points in the lecture and their relationship to the reading's points. A good essay will be 150 to 225 words.

Question: Summarize the points mentioned in the lecture. Be sure to explain how they cast doubt on the points mentioned in the reading passage.

As human population grows and cities expand, animals suffer from loss of habitats since their homes are destroyed by the construction of roads and buildings. A solution to rescue these animals have been proposed, which is to relocate the animals to a safe environment. However, there is mounting evidence that this method is not a practical solution.

To begin with, moving the animals to a new location can result in overpopulation. The new environment is already a home to a number of species with a balanced ecosystem and food scheme. With rescued animals moving in, there is bound to be overpopulation problems and animals will compete with one another for resource. This competition will lead to the demise of the animals since there will not be enough food, water, and living space. Therefore, the relocation solution may end up backfiring as the animals overcrowd and eventually starve to death from extreme competition.

Furthermore, relocating the animals may end up spreading unwanted disease to the new environment. Animals are carriers of many different diseases, so when they are moved to a new location, they unknowingly transport the diseases as well. This is a big problem because the animals in the new environment have never been exposed to the disease so they have little to no immunity. For example, there has been reported cases where endangered animals that were transported to the San Diego Zoo from mainland China carried mutated bird flu disease, so many of the animals in the zoo became sick.

Finally, there is a chance that animals may get injured and killed during the process of their capture. In order to move to a different location, animals must be captured first. Tranquilizer darts are used on the more massive and ferocious beasts, but at times, the dosage on the tranquilizers can be too much, which can lead to cardiac arrests on the animals that have been shot by it. Also, traps that have been set up to capture the animals may not provide adequate space and water once the animal is captured. When the trap captures the animal, sometimes it takes days for humans to retrieve it, but by the time they arrive, the animals have become dehydrated or suffered physical damage from confined space.

Essay

Writing for an Academic Discussion

For this part, you will read an online discussion. A professor has posted a question about a topic and two classmates have responded with their ideas. You have **10 minutes** to write.

Write a response that contributes to the online discussion. Use your own words in the response. Including memorized reasons or examples will result in a lower score. An effective essay will have a minimum of 100 words.

Click on the **Continue** button to go on.

Question 2 of 2

00:10:00

Your professor is teaching a class on social studies.
Write a post responding to the professor's question.

In your response you should:
- Express and support your opinion
- Make a contribution to the discussion

An effective response will contain at least 100 words.
You will have 10 minutes to write it.

Dr. Cox
When Ponce de Leon set out to find the Fountain of Youth, humanity's search for longevity began its quest. Unfortunately, no magical spring of eternal youth exists, so medicine and pharmaceutical drugs have increased life expectancies so that people can live longer lives. For an average person, a good diet and constant exercise is more than enough to prolong one's life. Which of these two do you think is more important? Why?

Elliot
These days, menus display how many calories are in the food diners order. This shows how much society emphasizes on good diet. There is a limit to how much calorie a person can consume, depending on their age, weight, and height. If they consume more calories than needed, they will become obese. Or, if they eat unbalanced meals, such as minimal fruits and vegetables and too much meat, then their health will deteriorate. So eating a good diet will prolong a person's life.

John
I go jogging every day. Sometimes I would play basketball after a light run. This shows how important exercise is for me. With constant exercise, people will stay fit, no matter how much they eat. After all, they can burn off their calories by going out for a run. Since I love to eat, I make sure to exercise every day so that I can live a healthy life.

Essay

Vocabulary:

expand	v.	become or make larger or more extensive.	*enlarge, swell*
suffer	v.	experience or be subjected to (something bad or unpleasant).	*hurt, ache*
propose	v.	put forward (an idea or plan) for consideration or discussion by others.	*suggest, offer*
relocate	v.	move to a new place and establish one's home or business there.	
mounting	adj.	grow larger or more numerous.	*increasing, rising*
scheme	n.	a large-scale systematic plan or arrangement for attaining a particular object or putting a particular idea into effect.	*plan, program*
demise	n.	the end or failure of an enterprise or institution.	*end, downfall*
backfire	v.	(of a plan or action) rebound adversely on the originator; have the opposite effect to what was intended.	*rebound*
carrier	n.	a person or animal that transmits a disease-causing organism to others. Typically, the carrier suffers no symptoms of the disease.	
expose	v.	cause someone to be vulnerable or at risk.	*subject*
immunity	n.	the ability of an organism to resist a particular infection or toxin by the action of specific antibodies or sensitized white blood cells.	*resistance to*
ferocious	adj.	savagely fierce, cruel, or violent.	*wild, rapacious*
cardiac arrest	n.	a sudden, sometimes temporary, cessation of function of the heart.	
adequate	adj.	satisfactory or acceptable in quality or quantity.	*sufficient, enough*
retrieve	v.	get or bring (something) back; regain possession of.	*recover, reclaim*
confined	adj.	(of a space) restricted in area or volume; cramped.	*cramped, restricted*
viable	adj.	capable of working successfully; feasible.	*feasible, practical*
barren	adj.	(of land) too poor to produce much or any vegetation.	*infertile, sterile*
artificial	adj.	made or produced by human beings rather than occurring naturally, especially as a copy of something natural.	*synthetic*
accommodate	v.	(of physical space, especially a building) provide lodging or sufficient space for.	*house, board*
inhabitant	n.	a person or animal that lives in or occupies a place.	*resident, dweller*
monitor	v.	observe and check the progress or quality of (something) over a period of time; keep under systematic review.	*observe, watch*
induce	v.	succeed in persuading or influencing (someone) to do something.	*persuade, convince*

Integrated Sample Essay

The reading passage claims that the rescuing of animals by relocating them to a safer habitat is not a practical solution. However, the listening passage argues that as long as proper procedures are carried out, relocating the animals is the most viable method.

To begin with, the writer claims that moving the animals to a new habitat will lead to overpopulation. Since the new environment is already a home to different species, organisms will compete with one another for resources and overpopulation will occur. The competition will lead to the extinction of animals since there will be minimal resources. On the other hand, the speaker contradicts this claim by stating that new habitats or increasing the capacity of the environment will solve the problem. Barren lands can be changed into habitats for organisms that do not require much plant and water, like desert reptiles and camels. So overpopulation will not be a problem. Also the carrying capacity of the environment can be increased through artificial methods. Artificial coral reefs have been used for a long time, helping fish and other marine o ganisms to adjust to a new home.

Furthermore, the author mentions that relocating animals will spread unwanted diseases to the new environment. Since animals are carriers of diseases, they will unknowingly transport the diseases to their new homes. Because the animals in the new habitat have never been exposed to the diseases, they will have no immunity. Conversely, the lecturer goes against this by stating that careful monitoring can prevent the spread of disease. When animals move to a new home, they can be placed in a separate area to prevent diseases from spreading. If experts notice anything wrong with the animals, they can move the species from the environment. Also, vaccines and shots can be given so that any known diseases will not be brought to the new environment.

Moreover, the text argues that there is a chance that the organisms will get injured or killed while being captured. In order to relocate, the animals must first be caught, but wrong tranquilizer dosage or inhospitable traps will cause more harm to the animals. On the contrary, the lecture challenges this argument by stating that injury and death can be prevented as well. Trap makers can make water dispensers inside the cages and GPS trackers can be attached to the cages to retrieve the animals. Also, instead of using chemical tranquilizers, people can use natural and herbal tranquilizers to induce the animal to sleep. Lemon balm, hops, and California poppy are some effective natural tranquilizers.

426 words

Academic Discussion Sample Essay

There are several factors that interplay to maintain a person's health. However, the most important aspect is a good diet. One should consume a balanced meal, with the appropriate amount of calories so that the body can function properly. As Elliot mentioned in her response, consuming too much calories will result in obesity. What's more, if the body is obese, they will have trouble even moving around and performing daily activities. This points to the fact that proper sustenance will allow exercise to be achieved, so it makes sense that a person should prioritize what they eat, more than how much exercise they perform. While strenuous exercise is recommended for longevity, individuals attain enough exercise from their daily chores. Cleaning the house, walking to school, or climbing the stairs is more than enough exercise. So it is essential that people eat well balanced meals.

144 words

Actual Test
02

Writing Section Directions

Make sure that the headset is turned on.

This section will measure your ability to use writing as a form of communication in an academic setting. There are two writing tasks.

For the first writing task, you will be reading a passage and listening to a lecture. Then you will answer a question based on what you read and listened to. For the second writing task, you will write an academic discussion essay answering a question posed by the professor, using your experience and knowledge.

Now listen to the directions for the first writing task.

Writing Based on Reading and Listening

For this part, you will have **3 minutes** to read an academic passage. Afterwards, the passage will disappear and you will listen to a lecture regarding the same topic. You are recommended to take notes on both the reading and the listening.

Afterwards, you will have **20 minutes** to write an essay summarizing the relationship between the reading passage and the lecture. Try to summarize as completely as possible using information from the reading passage and the lecture. This section of the writing does not ask you to write your personal opinion. You will see the reading passage again when it is time to write. You may use the notes you took to help write the essay.

A good essay will be 150 to 225 words long. Your response will be assessed on the quality of your writing and on the accuracy and completeness of the content from the reading and the lecture. If you finish your essay before the time is over, you may click **NEXT** to go to the next writing section.

Now, the reading passage will appear for 3 minutes. Remember, the reading passage will be available to you again when you are writing. When the 3 minutes is over, the lecture will begin right away, so keep your headset on until the lecture is finished.

Reading

Question 1 of 2

00:03:00

These days, environmentalists are greatly concerned with global warming. With rising temperatures across the globe, many sectors in our society have seen the damages caused by the climate change. Although some skeptics argue that global warming is not real, environmentalists argue that global warming is very real and can be seen in several areas.

First, higher sea levels indicate that the climate has increased in temperature. The glaciers that cover the north and south pole have witnessed a reduction in size, as it can be proven by satellite images that have taken pictures over a span of decades. For example, Antarctica has seen a loss of more than 3 trillion tons of ice in the past 25 years. The melting water from glaciers, as well as icebergs that have chipped off from glaciers, show that there has been a definite increase in temperature.

Second, global warming has induced severe weather events within the last few years. Within the United States, more frequent and massive tornadoes have swept across the central plains due to weather differences. In Southeast Asian countries, hurricanes and typhoons have created floods and torrential rain that swept away villages. In other parts of the world, snowstorms have trapped citizens in their homes, unable to go out due to the massive amounts of snow and ice. All of these weather events can only be brought forth from severe weather differences caused by global warming.

Third, the increase in global temperature has brought about food shortage. With the increasing temperature, certain parts of the world witnessed increased drought and minimal rain, which is unfortunate for farmers. With such unfruitful conditions, food production has reached an all-time low. Countries in Africa are especially suffering from global warming and many international relief groups are constantly providing food and water to these malnourished countries.

Listening

Question 1 of 2

(AT2.mp3)

Question 1 of 2

00:20:00

Directions: You have 20 minutes to organize and write your essay. Your essay will be assessed on the quality of your writing and how well you can summarize the points in the lecture and their relationship to the reading's points. A good essay will be 150 to 225 words.

Question: Summarize the points mentioned in the lecture. Be sure to explain how they cast doubt on the points mentioned in the reading passage.

These days, environmentalists are greatly concerned with global warming. With rising temperatures across the globe, many sectors in our society have seen the damages caused by the climate change. Although some skeptics argue that global warming is not real, environmentalists argue that global warming is very real and can be seen in several areas.

First, higher sea levels indicate that the climate has increased in temperature. The glaciers that cover the north and south pole have witnessed a reduction in size, as it can be proven by satellite images that have taken pictures over a span of decades. For example, Antarctica has seen a loss of more than 3 trillion tons of ice in the past 25 years. The melting water from glaciers, as well as icebergs that have chipped off from glaciers, show that there has been a definite increase in temperature.

Second, global warming has induced severe weather events within the last few years. Within the United States, more frequent and massive tornadoes have swept across the central plains due to weather differences. In Southeast Asian countries, hurricanes and typhoons have created floods and torrential rain that swept away villages. In other parts of the world, snowstorms have trapped citizens in their homes, unable to go out due to the massive amounts of snow and ice. All of these weather events can only be brought forth from severe weather differences caused by global warming.

Third, the increase in global temperature has brought about food shortage. With the increasing temperature, certain parts of the world witnessed increased drought and minimal rain, which is unfortunate for farmers. With such unfruitful conditions, food production has reached an all-time low. Countries in Africa are especially suffering from global warming and many international relief groups are constantly providing food and water to these malnourished countries.

Essay

Writing for an Academic Discussion

For this part, you will read an online discussion. A professor has posted a question about a topic and two classmates have responded with their ideas. You have **10 minutes** to write.

Write a response that contributes to the online discussion. Use your own words in the response. Including memorized reasons or examples will result in a lower score. An effective essay will have a minimum of 100 words.

Click on the **Continue** button to go on.

Question 2 of 2

00:10:00

Your professor is teaching a class on education.
Write a post responding to the professor's question.

In your response you should:
- Express and support your opinion
- Make a contribution to the discussion

An effective response will contain at least 100 words.
You will have 10 minutes to write it.

Professor Belding
Each year, universities are given funding and endorsement by the government and rich alumni in order to enhance their education. Still, schools lack financial resources to supplement their educational reforms. There are many areas that require funding: academic facilities like classrooms, equipment such as beam projectors, sports and athletic programs, and so much more. Where should universities prioritize their resources? Why?

Zack
The school should focus their resources on sports and athletic programs. These days, universities are popular for their sports teams. College football and basketball are shown on national television programs and people all over the United States tune in to watch their favorite college teams compete. If universities prioritize their funding on sports and athletic programs, more students will want to attend the school, which will boost the school image as well as financial profits.

Kelly
While I agree that classrooms are important, it would not be complete without proper equipment. A classroom is just a room. However, once it is furnished with high tech equipment like projectors, computers, and speakers, then professors and students alike will have an easier time teaching and learning the lesson. After all, a school should be a place to learn properly.

Essay

Vocabulary:

concerned	adj.	worried, troubled, or anxious.	*disturbed, bothered*
sector	n.	an area or portion that is distinct from others.	*section, zone*
skeptic	n.	a person inclined to question or doubt accepted opinions.	*cynic, pessimist*
witness	v.	see (an event, typically a crime or accident) take place.	*observe, watch*
reduction	n.	the action or fact of making a specified thing smaller or less in amount, degree, or size.	*depletion, cut*
span	n.	the full extent of something from end to end; the amount of space that something covers.	*period, time*
decade	n.	a period of ten years.	
drought	n.	a prolonged period of abnormally low rainfall, leading to a shortage of water.	*dry spell*
minimal	adj.	of a minimum amount, quantity, or degree; negligible.	*slightest, least*
unfruitful	adj.	not producing good or helpful results; unproductive.	*infertile, sterile*
relief	n.	assistance, especially in the form of food, clothing, or money, given to those in special need or difficulty.	*help, aid*
myth	n.	a widely held but false belief or idea.	*misbelief, fallacy*
exaggerate	v.	represent (something) as being larger, better, or worse than it really is.	*overstate, overstress*
misled	v.	cause (someone) to have a wrong idea or impression about someone or something.	*deceive, delude*
envelope	v.	to cover or contain a structure or layer.	*wrap, cover*
perish	v.	suffer death, typically in a violent, sudden, or untimely way.	*die, expire*
gradient	n.	an increase or decrease in the magnitude of a property (e.g. temperature, pressure, or concentration) observed in passing from one point or moment to another.	
outpace	v.	go, rise, or improve faster than.	*pass, outdo*

Integrated Sample Essay

The reading passage claims that global warming is very real and can be observed in several areas. However, the listening passage argues that the points mentioned in the reading are erroneous.

To begin with, the writer claims that higher sea levels point that the climate has increased in temperature. Glaciers have decreased in size, as satellite images in the duration of several decades is proof. The melting water from glaciers and the separation of icebergs from glaciers conclude that the temperature is on the rise. On the other hand, the speaker contradicts this claim by stating that humans are in a period called the post-ice age. Earth's history shows a repetition of ice age and melting period, and humans are in the no ice period. Even if another ice age comes about, the Earth will not turn into a ball of ice. The location of cities will move closer to the equator, since it is closer to the sun. So it is not global warming that is causing the water levels to rise, it is just a natural cycle the Earth is going through.

Furthermore, the author mentions that serious weather events have surfaced. In the United States, tornadoes have become more frequent and massive. Hurricanes, typhoons, and snowstorms have appeared more frequently from critical weather differences caused by global warming. Conversely, the lecturer goes against this by stating that the severe weather events are actually caused by man. Buildings have created a massive temperature gradient between the air and the ground. On a hot summer day, the asphalt can be as hot as 62 degrees Celsius, which can create tornadoes and other unnatural weather events. As long as humans create a less energy absorbent material for buildings and roads, unnatural weather phenomena will cease to exist.

Moreover, the text argues that global warming has brought food shortage. With higher temperatures, drought and minimal rain brought trouble to farmers. Food production has reached an all-time low. On the contrary, the lecture challenges this argument by stating that food shortage is a problem created by mankind. Human population increases exponentially, so the traditional methods of growing food is outpaced by the growing figures.These days, nontraditional methods, such as beverages that contain the nutrition of a single meal, have been produced to keep up with the growing numbers. Actually, this has become popular amongst those engaged in diet or trying to live a healthier lifestyle. So global warming has nothing to do with food shortage.

414 words

Academic Discussion Sample Essay

When resources are limited, it is important to know where one should prioritize in order to produce the most effective outcome. If a university needs to prioritize their resources, it is best that the school focuses on hiring and maintaining their professors. I agree with Zack that universities are popular for their sports teams. However, a university should be known for their academic programs and achievements. This can be accomplished by distinguished professors with prestigious backgrounds. For example, Ivy League schools such as Harvard or Yale are sought after by students all over the world. They wish to attend the school for its academic excellence, not to play football or basketball. The classes in these schools are taught by Nobel Prize candidates and professors with remarkable feats. Universities should make sure that their professors are satisfied with the working conditions and salary, and look to hire additional faculty who will contribute to the university. Thus, it is essential that the school focus their resources on their teaching staff.

168 words

Actual Test
03

Actual Test 03

Writing Section Directions

Make sure that the headset is turned on.

This section will measure your ability to use writing as a form of communication in an academic setting. There are two writing tasks.

For the first writing task, you will be reading a passage and listening to a lecture. Then you will answer a question based on what you read and listened to. For the second writing task, you will write an academic discussion essay answering a question posed by the professor, using your experience and knowledge.

Now listen to the directions for the first writing task.

Writing Based on Reading and Listening

For this part, you will have **3 minutes** to read an academic passage. Afterwards, the passage will disappear and you will listen to a lecture regarding the same topic. You are recommended to take notes on both the reading and the listening.

Afterwards, you will have **20 minutes** to write an essay summarizing the relationship between the reading passage and the lecture. Try to summarize as completely as possible using information from the reading passage and the lecture. This section of the writing does not ask you to write your personal opinion. You will see the reading passage again when it is time to write. You may use the notes you took to help write the essay.

A good essay will be 150 to 225 words long. Your response will be assessed on the quality of your writing and on the accuracy and completeness of the content from the reading and the lecture. If you finish your essay before the time is over, you may click **NEXT** to go to the next writing section.

Now, the reading passage will appear for 3 minutes. Remember, the reading passage will be available to you again when you are writing. When the 3 minutes is over, the lecture will begin right away, so keep your headset on until the lecture is finished.

Reading

Question 1 of 2

00:03:00

These days, schools require students to wear uniforms. In countries like South Korea and Japan, middle school and high school students are dressed in fashion and color that represent the school they attend. There are actually many advantages to wearing school uniforms.

First, wearing school uniforms ensures the safety of students. In crime ridden countries, school uniforms allow students to come to school without having to worry about gang fights or concealed weapons. Gangs are associated by specific colors, such as red, blue, or green, and wearing such bold colors indicate which gang the wearer belongs to. School uniforms conceal these colors and make sure there is no rivalry between gang members at school. Also, traditional casual clothes help conceal weapons underneath the baggy garments. However, since school uniforms are not loose, weapons can no longer be concealed and brought to school. Thus, safety at school is promised by wearing school uniforms.

Second, socioeconomic disparities are reduced by wearing school uniforms. Brand name clothes have become popular amongst teenagers in recent years. These brands range in several hundred dollars. A simple blue jean might cost $300 or a monotone sweater with a small mark on the chest might be worth $400. By wearing these clothing with a famous logo, students reveal their socioeconomic status and gaps will be created at school. Students who can afford such clothing will form their own groups and sometimes patronize and shun other students who cannot afford such clothes. A school uniform makes sure that everyone is seen equally and that such socioeconomic disparities do not exist.

Third, school uniforms promote academic studies. When students wear the same clothes every day to school, the time they save trying to figure out what to wear can be spent on studying for a quiz. Also, students will spend less time going out to shop for clothes, and so more time can be saved to study. At school, students will not worry about how they look since school uniforms look the same on everyone and so they can concentrate on what really matters, which is studying.

Listening

Question 1 of 2

(AT3.mp3)

Question 1 of 2

00:20:00

Directions: You have 20 minutes to organize and write your essay. Your essay will be assessed on the quality of your writing and how well you can summarize the points in the lecture and their relationship to the reading's points. A good essay will be 150 to 225 words.

Question: Summarize the points mentioned in the lecture. Be sure to explain how they cast doubt on the points mentioned in the reading passage.

These days, schools require students to wear uniforms. In countries like South Korea and Japan, middle school and high school students are dressed in fashion and color that represent the school they attend. There are actually many advantages to wearing school uniforms.

First, wearing school uniforms ensures the safety of students. In crime ridden countries, school uniforms allow students to come to school without having to worry about gang fights or concealed weapons. Gangs are associated by specific colors, such as red, blue, or green, and wearing such bold colors indicate which gang the wearer belongs to. School uniforms conceal these colors and make sure there is no rivalry between gang members at school. Also, traditional casual clothes help conceal weapons underneath the baggy garments. However, since school uniforms are not loose, weapons can no longer be concealed and brought to school. Thus, safety at school is promised by wearing school uniforms.

Second, socioeconomic disparities are reduced by wearing school uniforms. Brand name clothes have become popular amongst teenagers in recent years. These brands range in several hundred dollars. A simple blue jean might cost $300 or a monotone sweater with a small mark on the chest might be worth $400. By wearing these clothing with a famous logo, students reveal their socioeconomic status and gaps will be created at school. Students who can afford such clothing will form their own groups and sometimes patronize and shun other students who cannot afford such clothes. A school uniform makes sure that everyone is seen equally and that such socioeconomic disparities do not exist.

Third, school uniforms promote academic studies. When students wear the same clothes every day to school, the time they save trying to figure out what to wear can be spent on studying for a quiz. Also, students will spend less time going out to shop for clothes, and so more time can be saved to study. At school, students will not worry about how they look since school uniforms look the same on everyone and so they can concentrate on what really matters, which is studying.

Essay

Writing for an Academic Discussion

For this part, you will read an online discussion. A professor has posted a question about a topic and two classmates have responded with their ideas. You have **10 minutes** to write.

Write a response that contributes to the online discussion. Use your own words in the response. Including memorized reasons or examples will result in a lower score. An effective essay will have a minimum of 100 words.

Click on the **Continue** button to go on.

Question 2 of 2

00:10:00

Your professor is teaching a class on business management.
Write a post responding to the professor's question.

In your response you should:
- Express and support your opinion
- Make a contribution to the discussion

An effective response will contain at least 100 words.
You will have 10 minutes to write it.

Dr. Scott
With the onset of pandemics and long distance commute, remote work has become a standard working environment in various corporations and businesses across the world. Of course, this is still new for some people since it changes the way people work and interact with one another. Therefore, companies must consider all facets before making the decision to allow their workers to work in their homes. What is your opinion? Is remote work beneficial, or does it create more harm?

Jim
Remote work is definitely advantageous. For me, there are times when I finish the day's work in a few hours at the office. But since I'm obligated to stay at work, I get bored and waste my time playing around. However, working at home will allow me to spend that extra time productively by helping out with chores or even working for a side job.

Pamela
For me, remote work is still new. And I get scared of trying anything new. So working in the office is much better for me. Not only do you work, but you can have personal relationships with your coworkers. Since a person can spend several years working at the same job, I believe it is important to have relationships at work.

Essay

Vocabulary:

ridden	v.	be full of or dominated by.	*afflict, badger*
conceal	v.	keep from sight; hide.	*disguise, mask*
associate	v.	connect (someone or something) with something else in one's mind.	*relate, couple*
bold	adj.	(of a color or design) having a strong or vivid appearance.	*vivid, strong*
disparity	n.	a great difference.	*imbalance, inconsistency*
socioeconomic	adj.	relating to or concerned with the interaction of social and economic factors.	
monotone	adj.	without vividness or variety; dull.	*humdrum, routine*
patronize	v.	treat in a way that is apparently kind or helpful but that betrays a feeling of superiority.	*condescend, snub*
shun	v.	persistently avoid, ignore, or reject (someone or something) through antipathy or caution.	*avoid, evade*
loophole	n.	an ambiguity or inadequacy in the law or a set of rules.	
huddle	v.	crowd together; nestle closely.	*gather, herd*
imprint	v.	impress or stamp (a mark or outline) on a surface or body.	*mark, engrave*
alternative	adj.	(of one or more things) available as another possibility.	*another, possible*

Integrated Sample Essay

The reading passage claims that there are many benefits of wearing school uniforms. However, the listening passage argues that loopholes can be found in the points mentioned in the reading.

To begin with, the writer claims that school uniforms ensure safety. Uniforms allow students to come to school without worrying about gang fights nor hidden weapons. Uniforms will hide gang associated colors so there will be no rivalry between gang members at school. Also, school uniforms are not loose, so they will prevent weapons from being hidden and brought to school. On the other hand, the speaker contradicts this claim by stating that school uniforms actually do not conceal gang membership. Gangs will stay together in their own groups, which will help identify them. Also, gang tattoos will be visible when students wear short sleeved uniforms. Students will also have no trouble bringing weapons to school because they can place the weapons in hidden locations around the school the previous night when no one is there. So wearing uniforms do not prevent crime in school.

Furthermore, the author mentions that socioeconomic differences can be reduced. Brand name clothes can be several hundred dollars. By wearing such expensive clothes, students reveal their socioeconomic status and gaps will be made in school. School uniforms will make sure everyone is equal. Conversely, the lecturer goes against this by stating that socioeconomic differences will still be visible with uniforms. Shoes, backpacks, and accessories actually cost more than clothes, which cost more than a thousand dollars. The best method to hide socioeconomic gaps is for schools to provide shoes and backpacks, along with uniforms, so that not a single article of clothing will show their economic status.

Moreover, the text argues that uniforms help further academic studies. Students can save time every morning by not having to decide what to wear that day and they will spend less time shopping for clothes. This time saved can be invested in their studies. Even at school, students will not have to worry about how they look, since they will all look the same, so they will focus more on their studies. On the contrary, the lecture challenges this argument by stating that when students are wearing the same clothes, they will find other ways to stand out. Girls will put on more makeup and boys will style their hair differentl . This will require constant attention, so students will spend lots of time looking at mirrors and not focusing on their school work. Also, students will spend more time shopping because they will try to be more fashionable when they meet their friends outside of school. So students will spend less time on their studies.

447 words

Academic Discussion Sample Essay

People are used to clocking in to work and clocking out when their working hours are over. These days however, they can work in the comfort of their homes thanks to remote work. There are many benefits that this form of work can offer. First, precious time can be saved. Jim mentioned that he only works a few hours a day at the office. What's important is that employees must commute to work during rush hours. What could have been a thirty minute drive to work could end up being an hour if there is heavy traffic. Second, workers can spend more quality time for themselves or with their families. With people emphasizing on work life balance, employees can obtain this balance by working at home. They can take short breaks while working and spend time on their hobbies or talking with their loved ones. Therefore, there are more benefits to working remotely at home.

155 words

Actual Test
04

Actual Test 04

Writing Section Directions

Make sure that the headset is turned on.

This section will measure your ability to use writing as a form of communication in an academic setting. There are two writing tasks.

For the first writing task, you will be reading a passage and listening to a lecture. Then you will answer a question based on what you read and listened to. For the second writing task, you will write an academic discussion essay answering a question posed by the professor, using your experience and knowledge.

Now listen to the directions for the first writing task.

Writing Based on Reading and Listening

For this part, you will have **3 minutes** to read an academic passage. Afterwards, the passage will disappear and you will listen to a lecture regarding the same topic. You are recommended to take notes on both the reading and the listening.

Afterwards, you will have **20 minutes** to write an essay summarizing the relationship between the reading passage and the lecture. Try to summarize as completely as possible using information from the reading passage and the lecture. This section of the writing does not ask you to write your personal opinion. You will see the reading passage again when it is time to write. You may use the notes you took to help write the essay.

A good essay will be 150 to 225 words long. Your response will be assessed on the quality of your writing and on the accuracy and completeness of the content from the reading and the lecture. If you finish your essay before the time is over, you may click **NEXT** to go to the next writing section.

Now, the reading passage will appear for 3 minutes. Remember, the reading passage will be available to you again when you are writing. When the 3 minutes is over, the lecture will begin right away, so keep your headset on until the lecture is finished.

Reading

Question 1 of 2

00:03:00

Personal transportation has taken great strides with the advance in technology. Smarts cars utilize advanced engineering and computers with some form of artificial intelligence. Although smart cars have not yet shown their full potential, they are sure to show promising benefits in the near future.

One benefit smart cars will offer is help traffic flow faster. Since the smart car is driving itself, it will select optimal routes to arrive at the destinations, based on the number of cars and speed with which the routes will have. As a result, the travel will become much shorter and traffic will flow continuously. Also, human drivers are likely to make mistakes while driving. Sometimes they will doze off, which might lead to accidents and decrease the flow of traffic. Amateur drivers tend to drive below the speed limit, which will slow down the flow of traffic as well.

Furthermore, a smart car will have minimal maintenance costs. Smart cars alert drivers as soon as a minor problem surfaces. The owners will be able to take the car to a mechanic shop and fix the problem at a low cost before the minor problem develops into something more serious and more costly. Moreover, a smart car will handle the vehicle much better than a human driver, so tires, engines, or brake pads are less likely to wear out faster, so the car can be used for a longer period of time with minimal cost spent on repair.

Finally, smart cars run on lithium ion battery and do not rely on gasoline as fuel. As the planet has a finite source of fossil fuels to be used for gasoline, it is imperative that humans start to use decreasing amounts of it. Also, battery run smart cars do not produce any pollution. While cars running on gasoline release carbon to the environment which produces pollution, battery operated cars do not release anything that might harm the environment.

Listening

Question 1 of 2

(AT4.mp3)

Question 1 of 2

00:20:00

Directions: You have 20 minutes to organize and write your essay. Your essay will be assessed on the quality of your writing and how well you can summarize the points in the lecture and their relationship to the reading's points. A good essay will be 150 to 225 words.

Question: Summarize the points mentioned in the lecture. Be sure to explain how they cast doubt on the points mentioned in the reading passage.

Personal transportation has taken great strides with the advance in technology. Smarts cars utilize advanced engineering and computers with some form of artificial intelligence. Although smart cars have not yet shown their full potential, they are sure to show promising benefits in the near future.

One benefit smart cars will offer is help traffic flow faster. Since the smart car is driving itself, it will select optimal routes to arrive at the destinations, based on the number of cars and speed with which the routes will have. As a result, the travel will become much shorter and traffic will flow continuously. Also, human drivers are likely to make mistakes while driving. Sometimes they will doze off, which might lead to accidents and decrease the flow of traffic. Amateur drivers tend to drive below the speed limit, which will slow down the flow of traffic as well.

Furthermore, a smart car will have minimal maintenance costs. Smart cars alert drivers as soon as a minor problem surfaces. The owners will be able to take the car to a mechanic shop and fix the problem at a low cost before the minor problem develops into something more serious and more costly. Moreover, a smart car will handle the vehicle much better than a human driver, so tires, engines, or brake pads are less likely to wear out faster, so the car can be used for a longer period of time with minimal cost spent on repair.

Finally, smart cars run on lithium ion battery and do not rely on gasoline as fuel. As the planet has a finite source of fossil fuels to be used for gasoline, it is imperative that humans start to use decreasing amounts of it. Also, battery run smart cars do not produce any pollution. While cars running on gasoline release carbon to the environment which produces pollution, battery operated cars do not release anything that might harm the environment.

Essay

Writing for an Academic Discussion

For this part, you will read an online discussion. A professor has posted a question about a topic and two classmates have responded with their ideas. You have **10 minutes** to write.

Write a response that contributes to the online discussion. Use your own words in the response. Including memorized reasons or examples will result in a lower score. An effective essay will have a minimum of 100 words.

Click on the **Continue** button to go on.

Question 2 of 2

00:10:00

Your professor is teaching a class on education.
Write a post responding to the professor's question.

In your response you should:
- Express and support your opinion
- Make a contribution to the discussion

An effective response will contain at least 100 words.
You will have 10 minutes to write it.

Professor Cooper
Let's talk about the recent trend in education. Previously, a classroom included a physical space with chairs and tables, and students would sit down to receive their lesson. Nowadays, virtual classrooms exist thanks to the Internet, and students can learn in the comfort of their homes while immersing themselves onto their computer screens. My question is this. What is the most significant impact of online classes? Why?

Penny
Online classes have made interactions with classmates almost impossible. One of the best things about going to class physically was the interaction you could have with your classmates. Now that classmates meet online, there is no genuine interaction taking place. Even if text chat is available, the professor can turn the function off, rendering any interaction between classmates obsolete.

Leonard
The most significant impact online classes have given is the use of virtual tools to allow a more effective class. There are so many resources on the Internet that professors can use during the online class. Fun YouTube videos help grab students' attention in class, and there are interactive programs to stimulate science experiments or other activities students would not be able to do in a physical classroom due to hazardous implications. For example, during my online class in chemistry, my professor performed online experiments with chemicals that were unavailable at school and even showed how big explosions could get by mixing different chemicals.

Essay

Vocabulary:

potential	adj.	having or showing the capacity to become or develop into something in the future.	*possible, prospective*
promising	adj.	showing signs of future success.	*encouraging, hopeful*
optimal	adj.	best or most favorable; optimum.	*excellent, ideal*
doze off	v.	sleep lightly.	*nap, drowse*
amateur	n.	a person who is incompetent or inept at a particular activity.	*incompetent*
wear out	v.	be used until no longer in good condition or working order.	*deteriorate*
finite	adj.	having limits or bounds.	*limited, restricted*
imperative	adj.	of vital importance; crucial.	*vital, crucial*
bells and whistles		attractive additional features or trimmings.	
ease	v.	make (something) happen more easily; facilitate.	*facilitate, assist*
pedestrian	n.	a person walking along a road or in a developed area.	*walker, stroller*
instinct	n.	an innate, typically fixed pattern of behavior in animals in response to certain stimuli.	*inclination*
dominate	v.	have a commanding influence on; exercise control over.	*control, influence*
hazardous	adj.	risky; dangerous.	*dangerous, risky*
devastating	adj.	highly destructive or damaging.	*calamitous, cataclysmic*

Integrated Sample Essay

The reading passage claims that smart cars have several benefits for the future. However, the listening passage argues that smarts cars will not be so advantageous in the future.

To begin with, the writer claims that smart cars will help traffic to flow faster. Smart cars will choose the most optimal routes to arrive at their destinations, so travel time will decrease and there will be less traffic Also, human drivers are prone to make mistakes, as they can doze off while driving and create accidents, or amateur drivers can drive below the speed limit and slow down the traffic On the other hand, the speaker contradicts this claim by stating that smart cars will not help with traffic Because driving conditions are constantly changing, smart cars will encounter unexpected events while driving in its optimal route. Also, human instinct cannot be ignored when driving. Humans will use their experience and instinct to avoid roads that would have otherwise been troublesome.

Furthermore, the author mentions that smart cars will have few maintenance costs. Smart cars will alert drivers if something needs to be fixed, so drivers can solve the problem before it becomes a costly maintenance. Smart cars will also handle the cars better, so tires, engines, or brake pads will wear out slower so there will be less money spent on repairs. Conversely, the lecturer goes against this by stating that smart cars will not be cheap. Fixing the minor problems on smart cars are actually expensive since they do not dominate the market, their parts and repairs will be costlier than gasoline cars. Mechanics might have to import the parts because the smart cars are not as popular in the country. Also, replacing the battery will be as expensive as the car itself. Toyota's Prius contains a battery which is worth more than ten thousand dollars, compared to traditional car batteries worth less than a hundred dollars.

Moreover, the text argues that smart cars run on lithium ion battery, and not gasoline. This will save fossil fuels, which are a finite source. Also, smart cars will not create pollution since battery operated cars do not release anything that would harm the environment. On the contrary, the lecture challenges this argument by stating that lithium ion batteries of smart cars create hazardous wastes when the battery dies. When battery leakage occurs in these huge smart car batteries, the soil and groundwater will be polluted. Acid will leak out of the batteries and affect everything surrounding the battery. So a smart car battery actually creates harm in the environment.

429 words

Academic Discussion Sample Essay

Classes are no longer taught with pencils and paper. Education has evolved so that teachers and students can meet inside a virtual classroom. Although there are many bells and whistles to this novel method, the most significant impact of online classes is laziness amongst students. Like Penny said, one of the best memories I have in school is talking with my friends in class. While online classes prohibit such personal interaction, this made students to become lazy in their relationships as well. Instead of meeting a friend in person, individuals would rather chat with them online since it would be a hassle to get ready to go out. Furthermore, student are prone to skip online classes since the professor will not even check if the students are paying attention in an online classroom. Some people might not even attend the online lecture since they can ask someone to record the lecture so they can see it later. As students, they should be disciplined and responsible for keeping up with their lectures, even if the class is in an online classroom. Thus, the most significant impact of online classes is laziness.

190 words

Actual Test
05

Actual Test 05

Writing Section Directions

Make sure that the headset is turned on.

This section will measure your ability to use writing as a form of communication in an academic setting. There are two writing tasks.

For the first writing task, you will be reading a passage and listening to a lecture. Then you will answer a question based on what you read and listened to. For the second writing task, you will write an academic discussion essay answering a question posed by the professor, using your experience and knowledge.

Now listen to the directions for the first writing task.

Writing Based on Reading and Listening

For this part, you will have **3 minutes** to read an academic passage. Afterwards, the passage will disappear and you will listen to a lecture regarding the same topic. You are recommended to take notes on both the reading and the listening.

Afterwards, you will have **20 minutes** to write an essay summarizing the relationship between the reading passage and the lecture. Try to summarize as completely as possible using information from the reading passage and the lecture. This section of the writing does not ask you to write your personal opinion. You will see the reading passage again when it is time to write. You may use the notes you took to help write the essay.

A good essay will be 150 to 225 words long. Your response will be assessed on the quality of your writing and on the accuracy and completeness of the content from the reading and the lecture. If you finish your essay before the time is over, you may click **NEXT** to go to the next writing section.

Now, the reading passage will appear for 3 minutes. Remember, the reading passage will be available to you again when you are writing. When the 3 minutes is over, the lecture will begin right away, so keep your headset on until the lecture is finished.

Reading

Question 1 of 2

00:03:00

These days, it is rare to see someone not having a social media account. Social media records and displays people's daily lives for anyone to see and comment. There are many who are in favor that social media helps promote a sense of unity, create social interactions, and provide job opportunities to the millions of users who take advantage of it.

Social media instigates a sense of unity among the users. Whenever a politician steps in to argue against the citizens or encourages the passing of a law that might inflict certain members of society, people will come together and share their feelings on the web. News travel so fast these days that within mere seconds, people from the east coast of the United States will be aware of the injustice that is being served in the west coast. Social media users will unite under the same banner and their network will voice a strong opinion in the society.

Social interactions can be brought forth from social media. Some people have anxiety issues, where they cannot communicate normally with others like most people do. Under the veil of social media, these individuals can make friends online because they are protected by the computer screen and the distance that separates them from a nervous interaction. Also, love connections can be made online since people are so busy these days with work that they have no time go out and look for romantic relationships. In the past few years, dating websites have allowed romantic partners to meet and start a successful marriage.

Numerous jobs were provided by social media. Although social media sites like Facebook may look like a simple interface, as of June 2020, Facebook employs over 52,000 people. That is actually close to one third of the number of employees Microsoft employs, which is a high-end software computer company. Furthermore, people can share job openings with those who are in between jobs. Most companies like to hire people that their employees recommend instead of posting an advertisement on the job market. When the employee posts the job opening on the social media site, people can see the post and hopefully get the job.

Listening

Question 1 of 2

(AT5.mp3)

Question 1 of 2

00:20:00

Directions: You have 20 minutes to organize and write your essay. Your essay will be assessed on the quality of your writing and how well you can summarize the points in the lecture and their relationship to the reading's points. A good essay will be 150 to 225 words.

Question: Summarize the points mentioned in the lecture. Be sure to explain how they cast doubt on the points mentioned in the reading passage.

These days, it is rare to see someone not having a social media account. Social media records and displays people's daily lives for anyone to see and comment. There are many who are in favor that social media helps promote a sense of unity, create social interactions, and provide job opportunities to the millions of users who take advantage of it.

Social media instigates a sense of unity among the users. Whenever a politician steps in to argue against the citizens or encourages the passing of a law that might inflict certain members of society, people will come together and share their feelings on the web. News travel so fast these days that within mere seconds, people from the east coast of the United States will be aware of the injustice that is being served in the west coast. Social media users will unite under the same banner and their network will voice a strong opinion in the society.

Social interactions can be brought forth from social media. Some people have anxiety issues, where they cannot communicate normally with others like most people do. Under the veil of social media, these individuals can make friends online because they are protected by the computer screen and the distance that separates them from a nervous interaction. Also, love connections can be made online since people are so busy these days with work that they have no time go out and look for romantic relationships. In the past few years, dating websites have allowed romantic partners to meet and start a successful marriage.

Numerous jobs were provided by social media. Although social media sites like Facebook may look like a simple interface, as of June 2020, Facebook employs over 52,000 people. That is actually close to one third of the number of employees Microsoft employs, which is a high-end software computer company. Furthermore, people can share job openings with those who are in between jobs. Most companies like to hire people that their employees recommend instead of posting an advertisement on the job market. When the employee posts the job opening on the social media site, people can see the post and hopefully get the job.

Essay

Writing for an Academic Discussion

For this part, you will read an online discussion. A professor has posted a question about a topic and two classmates have responded with their ideas. You have **10 minutes** to write.

Write a response that contributes to the online discussion. Use your own words in the response. Including memorized reasons or examples will result in a lower score. An effective essay will have a minimum of 100 words.

Click on the **Continue** button to go on.

Question 2 of 2

00:10:00

Your professor is teaching a class on marketing.
Write a post responding to the professor's question.

In your response you should:
- Express and support your opinion
- Make a contribution to the discussion

An effective response will contain at least 100 words.
You will have 10 minutes to write it.

Dr. Stinson
Companies have used various methods to advertise to consumers. Nowadays, a new venue has become a popular method to advertise products and services: social media influencers. With the popularity of social media platforms, such as Instagram and YouTube, influencers have swayed consumer behavior with the products or services they display on social media. What do you think about this new marketing strategy? Why?

Marshall
I don't think social media influencers actually affect the purchasing behavior of consumers. People are smart enough to objectively critique a product or service without anyone telling them the merits since they base their decisions on their needs and preferences. Also, with so many influencers trying to promote different products and services, it becomes confusing for the consumers.

Lily
I depend on social media influencers when I purchase cosmetics or the latest gadget. Since influencers try on the makeup and provide helpful tips, I can rely on them for giving me the best products and tutorial on how to put them on. Also, I'm not much of a tech-person, so I look at YouTube clips that show influencers using various gadgets. After seeing them use the products, I feel more comfortable choosing what to buy.

Essay

Vocabulary:

rare	adj.	(of an event, situation, or condition) not occurring very often.	*infrequent, scarce*
promote	v.	further the progress of (something, especially a cause, venture, or aim); support or actively encourage.	*encourage, advance*
unity	n.	the state of being united or joined as a whole.	*coalition, federation*
instigate	v.	bring about or initiate (an action or event).	*incite, urge*
inflict	v.	cause (something unpleasant or painful) to be suffered by someone or something.	*impose, force*
mere	adj.	the smallest or slightest.	*scant, bare*
injustice	n.	lack of fairness or justice.	*corruption, brutality*
banner	n.	an idea or principle used to rally public opinion.	
flaw	n.	a fault or weakness in a person's character.	*defect, blemish*
anonymous	adj.	(of a person) not identified by name; of unknown name.	*nameless, unidentified*
fallacious	adj.	based on a mistaken belief.	*false, wrong*
appealing	adj.	attractive or interesting.	*attractive, alluring*
masculinity	n.	qualities or attributes regarded as characteristic of men.	*manliness*
aesthetic	adj.	concerned with beauty or the appreciation of beauty.	*ornamental, beautiful*
handful	n.	a small number or amount.	*few, some*
laid off	v.	fired	
con artist	n.	a person who cheats or tricks others by persuading them to believe something that is not true.	
naïve	adj.	(of a person or action) showing a lack of experience, wisdom, or judgment.	*innocent, inexperienced*

Integrated Sample Essay

The reading passage claims that social media provides several benefits to its users. However, the listening passage argues that social media should not be promoted in society.

To begin with, the writer claims that social media brings about a sense of unity amongst the users. Through social media, news travel quickly from one side of the country to the other. Social media users can unite and voice their opinion. On the other hand, the speaker contradicts this claim by stating that people coming together anonymously does not bring about unity. When people's identities are hidden, their opinions and actions do not matter. They will not even sign their names on petitions because they are afraid of their identities being revealed. For example, during the injustice of George Floyd, not even half the people who voiced their opinions on Facebook showed up to support the case.

Furthermore, the author mentions that social interactions can be achieved from social media. Some people have anxiety issues, so they can use social media to make friends online without having to encounter a nervous interaction. Also, romance can be matched since people can meet each other online. So even during their busy work schedule, love connections can be made which can lead to marriage. Conversely, the lecturer goes against this by stating that social interactions carried out in social media are lies. Individuals will make up fictitious information to make themselves more appealing. When falsely identified individuals meet in real life, they wil be disappointed.

Moreover, the text argues that many jobs are created by social media. A popular social media site, Facebook, actually employs three times the amount of people employed by Microsoft, an engineering company. Also, social media users can share job openings since companies prefer to hire people that their employees recommend instead of a random person from a job posting. On the contrary, the lecture challenges this argument by stating that jobs provided by social media carry risks. When social media companies grow, there is a chance that they will be bought out by a bigger company. When this occurs, people will lose their jobs because the bigger company will place their employees in the smaller company. Facebook purchasing Instagram and laying off hundreds of Instagram employees is just one example. Also, job postings on social media can be dangerous because con artists will steal personal information from people who upload their resumes.

402 words

Academic Discussion Sample Essay

The traditional methods of advertising have become archaic and consumers tend to rely on influencers. Still, no matter how hard social media influencers try to advertise products and services, I will never believe a word they say. I agree with Marshall that consumers are smart enough to judge for themselves if the product or service is worth purchasing. These days, consumers go to great lengths in researching the item they wish to buy. They will spend days comparing similar items in terms of cost and quality. I would also like to add that social media influencers should not be trusted. After all, they are getting paid by the company to advertise the product or service, so they will only comment on the positive aspects of the merchandise. Even if there is something they do not like, they will have to lie in order to satisfy the company that is paying them to advertise. Therefore, this new marketing strategy of utilizing social media influencers should not be trusted.

167 words

Answers and Script

Chapter 01
Integrated Essay Lesson

Page.12

통합형 에세이
통합형 에세이의 목표는 수험생이 리딩 지문과 강의에서 한 메모를 바탕으로 요약 에세이를 쓰는 것이다. 에세이는 구조화된 형식을 따라야 하며 리딩과 리스닝에서 나온 크고 작은 생각들을 요약할 수 있어야 한다.

시작하기 전에:
공책에 티차트를 그리고 한쪽에는 읽기라고 쓰고 다른 한쪽에는 듣기라고 쓴다. 각 측면은 작은 아이디어를 위한 공간을 사이에 두고 주제뿐만 아니라 3개의 요점을 가지고 있어야 한다. 수험생은 항상 조직화하여 메모해야 한다.

Page.13

리딩 메모:
수험생에게 한 구절을 읽고 주제, 요점, 작은 아이디어 등을 적는 시간이 3분 주어진다. 일부 수험생들은 이 모든 것을 적기에 충분한 시간이 없을 수도 있다. 따라서 타이머가 시작되고 읽기 지문이 나오는 순간, 이들의 눈은 읽기 지문의 4줄에 집중해야 한다.

샘플 지문:
인간과 동물은 수 천년 동안 서로 함께 살아왔다. 인간은 많은 다른 분야에서 자유뿐만 아니라 개인의 권리에 있어서 괄목할 만한 성장을 달성했다. 동물의 권리는 무시되어 왔고 인간이 이러한 작은 생물체들을 이용하기 때문에 계속해서 무시될 것이다.

인간이 동물을 사용하는 주된 장점은 약물 테스트에 있다. 우수한 종들이 건강하고 장수할 수 있도록 동물들은 약물 검사를 받는다. 어떤 질병과 바이러스는 실제로 동물들에게 투여된 다음, 개발된 약으로 치료되는데 이를 통해 인간들은 더욱 풍족한 삶을 살 수 있다. 동물 실험이 없다면, 신약과 개발 중인 약물은 인간에게 실험되어야 할 것이나, 대다수는 이를 거부할 것이다. 이와 같이 동물의 권리는 무시되어야만 인류가 더 건강해질 수 있다.

또 다른 이슈는 산업 발달로 인한 야생 동물들의 이동과 관련된 것이다. 인구는 기하급수적으로 증가하기 때문에 늘어나는 인구를 수용하기 위해서는 더 많은 주택과 인프라가 필요하다. 따라서 동물들이 땅과 물 위에 차지하는 공간이 파괴되어야만 건물과 도로가 만들어질 수 있다. 동물권이 보호된다면, 사람들은 비좁은 지역에서 살아야 할 것이고, 이것은 매우 불편하고 곤란할 것이다.

마지막으로, 강아지 사육장과 다른 불법 시설물들은 일반 시민들에게 저렴한 가격으로 고양이와 개를 제공한다. 최근 몇 년 동안, 애완동물 산업의 장은 커졌고 터무니없는 비용으로 고양이와 개의 특정 품종을 찾고 있다. 비록 우리에 갇힌 동물들은 인간 주인으로부터 사랑과 애정을 받지 못하지만, 그들의 자식은 사랑이 가득한 집으로 보내지고 건강한 환경에서 자라게 될 것이다. 이러한 애완 동물들에게 동물권을 주는 것은 애완동물 애호가들이 적당한 가격에 고양이나 개를 소유하는 선택권을 박탈할 것이다.

수험자의 메모는 다음과 같은 모습이어야 한다:

Page.14

The test taker's notes should look something like this:

R	L
주제: 동물권 X 왜냐하면 인간이 이익을 얻으므로	M: _____
1. 동물에 약물 실험 　동물이 실험에 이용되면 → 인간 건강 　질병 + 바이러스 주입 → 치료/신약	1: _____
2. 야생 동물 이동→산업 발달 　인구↑→더 많은 집 + 인프라 필요 　야생 동물 X 통해 건물 + 길 건설	2: _____
3. 강아지 사 + 지하 영업 → 저렴한 애완동물 　애완동물 사업 인기 → 애완동물 판매 　갇힌 동물들 그리고 사랑을 받지 못함	3: _____

메모는 약식이고 간결하다는 점에 유의하라. 수험생들은 메모에 문장을 적으며 시간을 낭비해서는 안 된다. 또한 일부 수험생에게는 작은 아이디어들을 적는 것이 어려울 수 있으므로 메모 순서는 다음과 같아야 한다.

　1) 주제
　2) 3개의 요점

　　시간이 남으면 요점 별로 2~3가지 세부사항을 적는다.
　　시험 응시자가 세부 사항을 적기에 충분한 시간이 없었으면 당황하지 말고 에세이를 쓸 때 다시 읽기 지문이 나타나므로, 그때 반드시 에세이에 세부 사항을 적어라.

ANSWERS AND SCRIPT

읽기 지문과 강의 사이의 관계 때문에 주제와 요점을 먼저 적는 것이 중요하다. 대부분의 경우, 강의는 읽기 지문에서 언급된 요점을 반박할 것이다. 그래서 읽기 지문의 주제와 요점을 이해함으로써, 강의를 듣기도 전에 무엇에 대해 토론할 지 짐작할 수 있다.

Page.16

리스닝 메모:
다음으로 수험생에게 듣기와 필기를 할 수 있는 2분의 강의가 주어진다. 읽기 지문과 달리 강의는 한 번만 진행되기 때문에 최소한의 세부 사항까지 포함해 가능한 한 많은 것을 적는 것이 중요하다. 여기에는 이름과 숫자가 포함된다.

샘플 강의:
이 읽기 지문은 동물의 권리가 무시되었고 인간이 동물로부터 얻는 많은 이점이 있기 때문에 계속해서 동물권이 무시될 것이라고 언급하고 있다. 그러나, 이 읽기 지문은 실제로 동물권이 글에서 언급된 분야에서 적용되고 있다는 것을 간과했다.

약물 테스트와 관련하여, 물론 동물들은 동물이 아닌 사람에게 혜택을 주는 개발 약으로 치료된다. 하지만, 이 실험에서는 동물의 안녕이 우선시된다. 예를 들어, 침팬지에게 새로운 약물을 투여하고 그들이 원치 않는 부작용의 작은 징후가 나타나면, 침팬지들에게는 항생제와 다른 승인된 약물이 주어진다. 동물의 권리를 고려하지 않았다면 침팬지는 아무런 치료도 받지 못하고 죽게 내버려졌을 것이다.

게다가, 인간이 야생 동물 서식지에 도로와 건물을 지을 때, 그들은 동물들이 피난처로 삼고 돌아갈 수 있도록 땅의 일부를 그대로 둔다. 건설사들은 사실상 특정 지역을 내버려둔 채 기반 시설을 만들 의무가 있다. 또한, 집 없는 동물들이 새로운 서식지를 만들 수 있도록 땅과 건물을 설치하는 민간 단체들도 있다. 따라서, 인간들이 살 집을 만드는 동안, 집에 대한 그들의 권리는 실제로 보존되고 있다.

마지막으로, 강아지 사육장과 다른 불법 영업장들의 끔찍한 상태는 과거에 많은 사람들의 눈살을 찌푸리게 했다. 하지만, 요즈음 강아지 사육장들은 동물들이 건강하고 위생적인 상태로 지낼 수 있도록 동물 권리 운동가들이 설정한 조건을 따른다. 이 사육장 안에 있는 동물들에게는 밖으로 나갈 수 있는 놀이 시간이 주어지고 매일 보충제를 먹인다. 동시에, 새끼들은 애완동물 애호가에게 양도되기 전에 어미로부터 양육될 충분한 시간이 주어진다. 그래서 다시 말하지만, 강아지 사육장과 관련 시설 내에서 동물 권리는 지켜진다.

Page.18

기억할 것 : 할 수 있는 한 세부 사항을 많이 적어라. 글을 많이 쓰면 쓸수록 좋다. 토플 통합형 에세이는 상대적 척도로 등급이 매겨지는데, 다른 사람이 쓸 수 없는 것을 쓰면 더 높은 점수를 받는 반면 다른 사람은 더 낮은 점수를 받는다는 것을 의미한다.

보다시피, 강의 노트는 리딩 지문이 언급하는 내용과 정면으로 배치된다. 드문 경우이긴 하지만, 이 관계는 다를 수 있다. 이러한 드문 경우로는 다음과 같은 경우가 있다.

의문 제기
주어진 예시도 의문을 제기하는 형식이긴 하지만, 리딩과 강의가 모두 하나의 의견(동물권이 보호 되어야 하는가 아닌가)에 초점을 맞췄다. 그러나 주제에 대해 세 가지 다른 의견을 제시하는 경우도 있다. (철갑상어가 뛰는 세 가지 목적)

문제 및 해결책
리딩 지문은 주제를 소개하고 세 가지 문제를 제시한다. 이와 대조적으로, 교수자는 각각의 문제에 대해 세 가지 해결책을 제안할 것이다.

Page.20

템플릿을 모두 다 암기해야 하는 것은 아니다; 그러나 시험 응시자는 에세이의 구조에 대해 반드시 이해하고 있어야 한다.

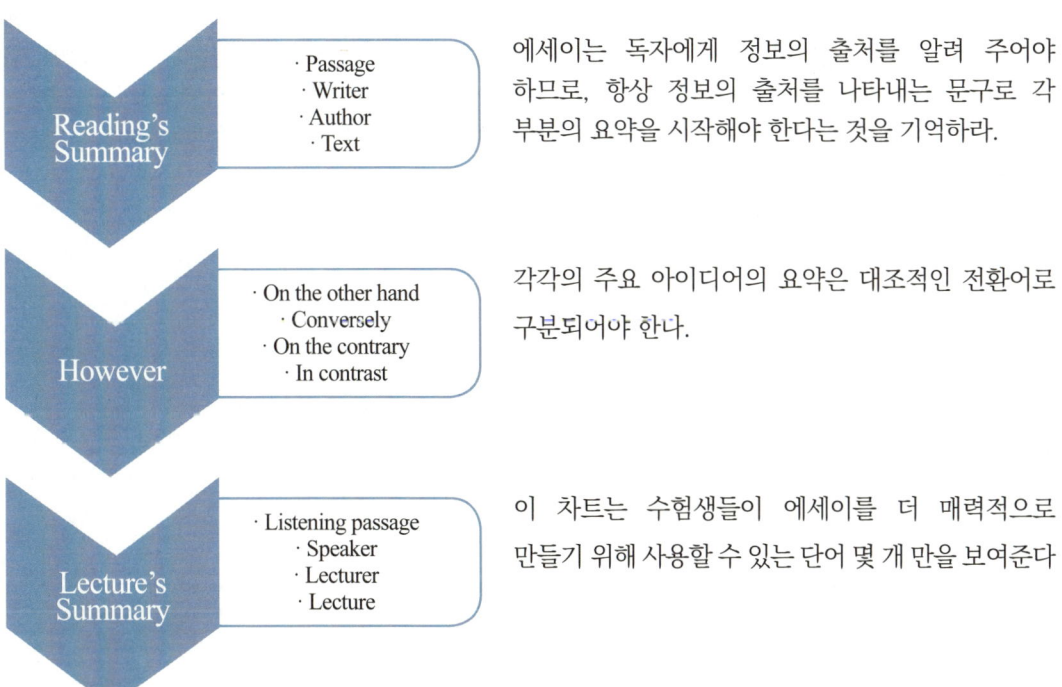

에세이는 독자에게 정보의 출처를 알려 주어야 하므로, 항상 정보의 출처를 나타내는 문구로 각 부분의 요약을 시작해야 한다는 것을 기억하라.

각각의 주요 아이디어의 요약은 대조적인 전환어로 구분되어야 한다.

이 차트는 수험생들이 에세이를 더 매력적으로 만들기 위해 사용할 수 있는 단어 몇 개 만을 보여준다

ANSWERS AND SCRIPT

Page.21

샘플 에세이

읽기 지문은 동물의 권리를 이용하는 인간 때문에 동물의 권리가 지속적으로 무시되고 있다고 설명한다. 그러나 듣기 지문은 동물의 권리가 실제로 보호되고 있다고 주장한다.

우선, 저자는 약품들이 동물들에게 실험되고 있고, 그것이 동물들의 권리를 침해한다고 주장한다. 그 실험은 동물들의 이익을 위해서가 아니라 인간의 건강을 위해서 동물들에게 행해지는 것이다. 때로는 동물들에게 바이러스 주사를 놓거나 질병에 노출시킨 뒤, 제약 회사가 개발 중인 신약으로 치료하기도 한다. 반면, 강사는 동물의 안녕이 제약 회사의 최우선 순위라고 말하면서 이 주장에 반박한다. 예를 들어 침팬지들을 신약으로 실험해 원치 않는 부작용을 보이면 즉시 통증을 치료하는 치료를 제공한다. 만약 동물의 권리가 무시되고 있었다면, 실험 대상 동물들은 죽게 내버려 두었을 것이다.

게다가, 저자는 인간이 산업 발전을 위해 야생 동물 서식지를 대체하고 있다고 말한다. 인구가 지속적으로 증가함에 따라, 인간은 증가하는 인구를 수용할 수 있는 더 많은 주택과 인프라가 필요하다. 인간이 더 많은 건물과 도로를 만들수록 동물들은 무시되고 있다. 반면에 강사는 도로와 건물을 건설하면서도, 일부 토지는 손대지 않은 채 남겨 두었다고 반박한다. 건설 회사들은 사실상 법에 의해 토지의 일부를 손대지 않은 채 남겨 둘 의무가 있다. 또한, 민간 단체들은 집을 잃은 동물들을 위해 땅과 건물을 지었다. 따라서, 서식지에 대한 동물의 권리는 보존되고 있다.

게다가, 본문은 강아지 번식장과 다른 불법 시설물이 애완동물을 기르고 싶어하는 사람들에게 값싸게 애완동물을 제공한다고 주장한다. 최근 반려동물 산업이 인기를 끌면서 반려동물이 고가에 팔리고 있다. 동물들은 우리에 갇혀 사랑을 받지 못하는 반면, 그들은 싼 가격에 팔기 위해 강제로 새끼를 낳는다. 반대로 강사는 강아지 번식장이 실제로 동물 권리 활동가들이 정한 조건을 따른다고 밝혀 이 주장에 반박한다. 그 동물들은 건강하고 위생적인 환경에서 살고 있다. 그들에게는 밖에서 놀 수 있는 시간이 주어지고 매일 보충제를 먹인다. 또한, 새끼들은 애완동물 주인들에게 팔리기 전에 엄마의 보살핌을 받는다.동물들을 위해 땅과 건물을 지었다. 따라서, 서식지에 대한 동물의 권리는 보존되고 있다.

Page.22~23

공식 토플 시험에서 통합형 논술의 단어 수는 150~225단어 사이이다. 그러나, 메모의 양으로는, 225단어 안에 모든 정보를 담는 것은 불가능하다. 따라서 사소한 점뿐만 아니라 모든 핵심 내용을 담은 읽기와 듣기 내용을 담고 있는 에세이는 300단어 이상의 단어 수를 가져야 한다. 당신은 더 긴 에세이를 써야 하는 점에서 감점되지 않을 것이다.

기억하라, 수험생에게는 에세이를 타이핑할 수 있는 시간이 20분밖에 주어지지 않기 때문에 타이핑 속도가 느리면, 연습을 해야만 완벽해질 수 있다. 연습을 재미있게 하기 위한 온라인 타이핑 게임이 다수 존재한다.
에세이를 편집하는 것을 잊지 마라. 편집은 에세이 쓰기 과정의 일부분이다. 타이머가 끝날 때, 편집을 마쳐야 잘했다고 할 수 있다.

왜 통합형 에세이에서 낮은 점수를 받는가?

1) 정보 부족 : 통합논술의 목적은 리딩과 리스닝을 요약하는 것이다. 수험자는 이름과 숫자와 같은 작은 세부 사항을 포함하여 크고 작은 아이디어를 제시해야 한다.

2) 잘못된 정보 : 수험생이 에세이를 쓰는 공간 옆에 본문이 나타나기 때문에 리딩에서 잘못된 정보를 쓰기는 거의 어렵다. 틀린 정보는 리스닝(강의)에서 나오는데, 이 강의에서 수험생이 특정 정보를 잘못 듣고 틀린 내용을 적어둔 것이다.

3) 새로운 정보 : 간혹 수험생들은 리딩이나 리스닝에 언급되지 않은 정보를 적는 경향이 있다. 배경 지식에서 얻을 수 있는 정보는 포함하지 않도록 한다.

4) 단어 그대로 복사 : 리딩 구절을 복사하지 않는다. 동의어를 사용하고 문장 구조를 변경하여 자신만의 언어로 정보를 서술하라.

5) 조직화 : 에세이의 구성이 먼저 읽히고, 그 다음에 대조적인 단어, 그 다음에 리스닝 요약이어야 한다는 것을 기억하라.

6) 오타와 문법 실수 : 수험생들이 할 수 있는 가장 실망스러운 실수 중 하나는 단어의 철자를 틀리는 것이다. 그러나 이들이 적는 말은 글쓰기 코너 옆 리딩 본문에 나타나기 때문에 간과될 수 없다. 문법 실수는 사실상 식별이 어렵다. 문법이 서툰 사람은 자신의 실수를 확인할 수 없기 때문이다.

ANSWERS AND SCRIPT

Chapter02
Integrated Essay Lesson

Page.28

연습1
오늘날, 사람들은 자유 시장 체제 입장을 추구한다. 자유 시장 경제학자들은 정부의 간섭이 미미하거나 거의 없는 시장이 개인과 정부 기관 모두에게 가장 유익하다고 믿는다. 자유 시장 자본주의가 유리한 선택임을 증명하는 세 가지 요소가 있다.

자유 시장 자본주의는 많은 나라에서 안정적이라는 것이 증명되었다. 예를 들어, 미국에서는 경제 침체에도 불구하고, 특히 대공황 기간 동안에도 자유 시장 제도가 지속되었다. 정부 기관들은 경제적 어려움을 다루는데 있어서 형편없는 선택을 했고, 자유 시장 자본가들만이 그들의 사업에 있어 어떠한 변동도 없음을 입증하였다. 개인은 비상 시에 신속하게 행동하기 때문에 이익 손실을 보지 않게 된다. 이러한 신속한 대응을 통해 자유 시장 자본가들은 많은 다른 나라들에서 강세를 유지해 왔다.

자유 시장 체계에서는 민족이나 배경을 불문하고 개인이 창업에서 성공할 수 있는 동등한 기회를 가진다. 성공적인 신화들은 누구나 성공할 수 있다는 것을 증명했다. 페이스북 창업자인 마크 저커버그와 애플을 전자 제품계의 거물로 만든 고 스티브 잡스는 둘 다 초라한 배경에서 나왔으나 그들의 아이디어와 사업에서 성공을 거뒀다. 만약 정부가 그들의 일에 관여했다면, 국민들은 소셜 네트워크 연결도, 우리가 즐기는 미적으로 설계된 장치도 갖지 못했을 것이다. 그래서 정부 자유 시장은 누구나 각자의 분야에서 성공할 수 있도록 한다.

마지막으로, 경제에 대한 정부의 개입은 실제로 경제 내에서의 호황과 불황을 일컫는 경기 순환의 원인이 되기도 한다. 정부가 소비자의 수요에 응하지 않거나 장기적으로 지속 가능하지 않은 기업을 대상으로 자원을 잘못 배분하게 될 때, 시장 불안을 조성하고 악명 높은 경기 순환을 만들어낸다.

Practice1 Page.30

Integrated Practice 1
(Female Professor)
The author of the reading believes that free market enterprise is the better option, however, a government-run market is actually more favorable. The government is most appropriate to hand out economic resources through infrastructure projects and social programs.
Although the United States does benefit from a free market system in terms of stability, the rest of the world does not share the same opinion. Most countries around the world have a system set up where

the government is involved at least partially in the market system. A government's goal is for the country to prosper, so it will do everything in its power to make sure it achieves that goal. Individuals can become greedy and power thirsty, so even a small mistake due to gluttony can lead to a collapse of a market which plays a powerful hand in their country's economy.

Furthermore, government interference is necessary for the sake of equal opportunities. In an ideal state, everyone should be given equal chance. However, the world we live in is controlled by those with power and those with power remain strong while those who are weak stay weak. This solid rule applies in the market as well, as those with money will make more money. The government should therefore involve itself in such matters so that even those who have no money or prestigious background can still succeed in the market.

Finally, advocates of a government regulated market system believe that the business cycle can be prevented with government involvement. Individuals calling themselves the Keynesians believe that the government should control the free markets through fiscal policy, such as taxing, borrowing, and spending, and monetary policy, which include printing money and setting the interest rate. This will help prevent the ugly business cycle and also prevent economic recessions.

이 글의 저자는 자유 시장 기업이 더 나은 선택이라고 생각하지만 실제로는 정부가 개입하는 시장이 더 유리하다. 정부가 인프라 사업과 사회적 프로그램을 통해 경제 자원을 분배하는 것이 가장 적절하다. 미국이 비록 안정이라는 측면에서 자유 시장 체제의 혜택을 누리고 있지만, 세계의 나머지 국가들이 같은 의견을 공유하는 것은 아니다. 세계 대부분의 나라들은 최소한 정부가 부분적으로나마 시장 시스템에 관여하는 시스템을 갖추고 있다. 정부의 목표는 나라가 번영하는 것이기 때문에, 정부는 그 목표를 달성하도록 하기 위해 온 힘을 다할 것이다. 개인은 탐욕스럽고 권력에 갈증을 느낄 수 있기 때문에, 탐욕에 의한 작은 실수라도 자국 경제에 막강한 힘을 발휘하는 시장의 붕괴로 이어질 수 있다.

더 나아가, 정부의 간섭은 기회 균등을 위해 필요하다. 이상적인 상태에서는 모든 사람에게 동등한 기회가 주어져야 한다. 그러나 우리가 살고 있는 세상은 권력을 가진 자에 의해 지배되고 권력을 가진 자들은 강한 상태를 유지하는 반면 약한 자들은 약한 상태로 머물러 있다. 이 확실한 규칙은 시장에서도 적용되는데, 왜냐하면 돈을 가진 사람들은 더 많은 돈을 벌 것이기 때문이다. 따라서 정부는 돈이 없는 사람들이든, 일류 배경을 가진 사람들이든 시장에서 성공할 수 있도록 그러한 문제에 관여해야 한다.

마지막으로, 정부 규제를 받는 시장 시스템의 옹호자들은 정부 개입이 경기 순환을 막을 수 있다고 믿는다. 스스로를 케인즈주의자라고 부르는 사람들은 정부가 세금, 차입, 지출 등의 재정 정책과 조폐, 금리 설정 등의 통화 정책을 통해 자유 시장을 통제해야 한다고 본다. 이는 안 좋은 경기 순환을 막고 또한 경기 침체를 막는데도 도움이 될 것이다.

Practice2 Page.36

연습2

많은 학교와 연구 기관들이 교육용 비디오와 녹화에 더 많이 의존하기 시작하고 있다. 전통적인 교육자들은 교과서를 이용해 스스로 수업을 하는 것을 선호하지만, 교육 미디어에 대한 의존은 사실상 긍정적인 추세이다.

학생들은 미디어 자료에서 시각적 도움을 받아 더 많이 집중하는 경향이 있다. 21세기는 교육을 비롯한 여러 분야에서 시각적인 영향력이 함께하는 시대다. 학생들은 교과서를 읽는 것보다 비디오를 보는 것에 더 익숙하다. 시각적 도구를 통해 교사들은 학생들의 관심을 끌 수 있는 더 큰 기회를 가질 수 있다. 또한, 교사들은 차트와 애니메이션을 통해 학생들에게 어려운 개념을 더 쉽게 설명하게 될 것이다. 이것은 학생들이 더 잘 이해하는데 도움을 줄 것이고, 이것은 학생들의 교육 진보를 돕는 확실한 장점이 될 것이다.

또한 교육 미디어는 교사나 교과서보다 훨씬 더 싸다. 일회성 수업을 위해 교사를 고용하는 것은 교육용 비디오를 통해 가르치는 것보다 몇 배 더 비싸다. 또한, 교과서는 100달러 이상의 비용이 들 수 있는 반면, 교육용 DVD는 10달러 미만이 될 수 있다. 교실 당 DVD하나씩을 구입하는 대신 학교에서 DVD 사본 한 장만 구입하면 되기 때문에 교육비를 최소화할 수 있다. 학생과 학교는 계속되는 빠듯한 예산으로 항상 정부 지원을 요청하고 있다. 교육용 미디어를 구입함으로써, 학생들과 학교들은 많은 돈을 절약할 수 있고, 이것은 그들이 다른 중요한 물품들을 구입하는데 사용할 수 있다.

마지막으로 교육 매체는 더 넓은 그룹의 학생들에게 교육에 대한 접근을 제공할 것이다. 미국과 같은 나라들은 보통 교육으로부터 혜택을 받지만, 아시아와 아프리카와 같은 제3세계 국가들에는 아이들이 다닐 학교가 없다. 만약 이 아이들이 교육 매체를 접할 수 있게 된다면, 그들은 집에서 편안하게 그들의 나이에 필요한 교육을 받을 것이다. 어떤 아이도 교육적 매체의 사용에서 뒤쳐지지 않을 것이다.

Practice2 Page.38

Integrated Practice 2
(Male Professor)
I know that a lot of you watch educational videos to help supplement the lessons that you learned here at school. But educational videos are exactly that: supplementary materials. They will never be able to replace traditional classrooms for the following reasons.
To begin with, educational videos are limited by time. There is only so much information that can be delivered in a one-hour video. With the limitation of time, the lesson will be incomplete and not have all the important details, so the student will be left with unanswered questions. However, a textbook is filled with a plethora of information enough to answer any questions students might have. In addition, educational media are designed to entertain than educate. This means that the lessons are highly simplified. You cannot explain difficult concepts on media since the viewers will lose interest and not pay attention.

Furthermore, educational media really are not that cheap compared to teachers and books. In most cases, videos of movies are cheap, however, this is not the case for educational media. They are very costly since education in whatever format is expensive and these media are meant to help you succeed in life. Also, in order to watch the educational videos, students must first purchase either a DVD player or a computer, which is not cheap. If the computer happens to malfunction, fixing the machine will be expensive. These days, educational videos are offered online, which require internet access that needs to be paid on a monthly term.

Moreover, educational video will be limited to the number of people they can reach out to. For example, families with low income will not be able to afford computers to watch educational media. Even in countries like America, there are families who do not own computers at home. In third world countries like Asia and Africa, villages will often own one television set or computer so children will be limited from accessing the educational media. Unfortunately, these children are spending most of their time working in factories so they will not have the time to study. As such, even with educational media, the people who have access to it will be limited.

나는 여러분 대부분이 학교에서 배운 수업 내용을 보충하기 위해 교육용 비디오를 시청한다는 것을 알고 있다. 그러나 교육용 비디오는 정확하게는 보충 자료이다. 그것들은 다음과 같은 이유로 결코 전통적인 교실을 대체할 수 없을 것이다.

먼저, 교육용 동영상은 시간에 따른 제약이 있다. 한 시간짜리 동영상으로 전달될 수 있는 정보는 한계가 있다. 시간의 제약으로, 수업은 불완전하고 중요 세부사항까지 모두 전달하지 못하기 때문에, 학생들은 풀리지 않은 질문을 가지게 될 것이다. 하지만, 교과서는 학생들이 가질 만한 어떤 질문에도 답할 수 있을 만큼의 많은 정보들로 채워져 있다. 게다가, 교육 미디어는 교육보다 즐거움을 주기 위해 고안되었다. 이는 학습이 고도로 단순화되었다는 것을 의미한다. 미디어에서는 어려운 개념을 설명할 수 없는데, 이는 시청자들이 흥미를 잃고 주의를 기울이지 않을 것이기 때문이다.

더 나아가, 교육 매체는 교사의 강의나 책에 비해 그다지 경제적이지 않다. 대부분의 경우, 비디오 영화는 저렴하지만, 교육 매체는 그렇지 않다. 어떤 형식의 교육이든 비용이 많이 들기 마련이고, 이러한 미디어는 인생에서 당신이 성공하도록 도와주기 위한 것이기 때문에 매우 비싸다.

또한, 교육용 비디오를 시청하기 위해서는, 학생들은 DVD 플레이어나 컴퓨터를 먼저 구입해야 하는데, 이것은 저렴하지 않다. 만약 컴퓨터가 오작동 한다면, 고치는 비용이 많이 들 것이다. 요즘은 교육용 동영상이 온라인으로 제공되고 있는데, 이를 위해서는 매달 비용을 지불해야 하는 인터넷 접속이 필요하다.

게다가, 교육용 비디오는 접근할 수 있는 사람들의 숫자에 제약이 있을 것이다. 예를 들어, 저소득층 가정은 교육용 미디어를 시청할 컴퓨터를 구입할 여유가 없을 것이다. 심지어 미국과 같은 나라에서도 집에 컴퓨터를 가지고 있지 않은 가정이 있다. 아시아와 아프리카와 같은 제3세계 국가에서는, 마을에 종종 한 대의 텔레비전이나 컴퓨터만을 소유할 것이기 때문에 어린이들이 교육용 미디어에 접근하는 것에는 제약이 따를 것이다. 안타깝게도, 이 아이들은 대부분의 시간을 공장에서 일하면서 보내고 있기 때문에 공부할 시간이 없을 것이다. 그런 만큼 교육용 매체를 사용하더라도 이에 접근할 수 있는 사람은 제한적일 수밖에 없다.

ANSWERS AND SCRIPT

Practice3 Page.44

연습3

여러 해 동안 음악 교육은 미국 학교 교과 과정의 일부가 되었다. 일부 교육 전문가들은 모든 학생들이 계속해서 음악을 공부해야 한다고 믿는다. 하지만, 의무적인 음악 수업이 몇 가지 문제가 있다고 믿는 사람들이 있다.

첫째, 음악 수업은 학생들이 사회에서 현실적인 직업을 가질 수 있게끔 준비시키지 않는다. 대다수의 학생들은 과학, 사업, 또는 기술 분야의 직업을 추구할 것이다. 학생들이 음악 수업에서 무엇을 배우든 간에 그들의 미래 직업에 도움이 되지 않을 것이다. 학교에 다니는 목적은 정보를 배우고 나중에 그들에게 도움이 될 경험을 쌓는 것이다. 수학 강좌, 과학 강좌 등은 학생들에게 실용적일 수 있는 귀중한 정보를 제공한다. 그러므로, 학생들은 음악 수업을 듣지 말아야 한다. 왜냐하면 그 수업들이 그들의 미래 직업에 거의 도움이 되지 않기 때문이다.

둘째, 이러한 수업에서 학생들을 평가하고 성적을 주는 것은 불공평하다. 선천적으로 음악에 재능이 없는 학생도 있다. 때때로 그들은 음치일 수 있다. 비록 어떤 사람들은 연습이 완벽을 만든다고 말할지 모르지만, 몇 년 동안 연습한 것이 완벽하지 않은 경우도 있다. 이런 학생들은 음악 수업에서 낙제할 가능성이 높은 반면, 음악에 타고난 재능이 있는 학생들은 성공할 것이다. 좋은 대학에 들어가거나 취업을 하기 위해서는 내신 성적이 필수적이기 때문에 학생부 성적표에 남은 낙제점은 학생들에게 전혀 도움이 되지 않는다.

셋째, 악기는 비싸다. 바이올린은 수백 달러가 들 수 있고 플루트나 클라리넷도 마찬가지로 비쌀 수 있다. 저소득 가정 출신 학생들에게는 이렇게 비싼 악기를 구입하는 것이 큰 부담이 될 수 있다. 또한, 악기를 유지하는 것도 비용이 많이 든다. 바이올린 현은 몇 달 사용 후에, 클라리넷에 사용되는 리드는 몇 주 후에 교체해야 한다. 악기가 파손될 경우 수리하는 비용도 무시할 수 없다.

Practice3 Page.46

Integrated Practice 3
(Female Professor)
So, the reading passage talks about some interesting problems mandatory music classes bring to the school system. In reality, music classes provide numerous benefits in and outside of school, so the problems mentioned in the reading are non-existent.
The reading argues that music classes are useless in preparing students for their future careers. However, music classes help stimulate students to perform better in other classes. Music classes teach rhythms and theories, which can be applied in math classes as well as certain science courses. Also, the highlight of a music class is for students to make music, expanding their own limits in imagination. This can help students when they are writing creative essays in literature classes or making nontraditional projects at school. With the lessons learned in music classes, students can improve their performance in other areas, which will help them get good scores and allow them to

enter the university of their choice and get a good job.

In regards to unfair grading in music classes, just because a student is attending a music class does not mean their entire grade is based on how well they can make music. Their overall grade is determined by class attendance, participation, musical theory comprehension, and reports. Even if a student is tone deaf or does not have the natural playing skills to hold an instrument, their hard work will result in getting a passing score in the class. So, students should not be discouraged from taking the class just because they have no musical talent.

Although musical instruments are expensive, there are many solutions to help overcome this problem. These days, violins and flutes are manufactured in great quantities since they are in high demand. This has also led to decreased costs since the instruments are made in bulk. Unless a student wants a handcrafted instrument, these manufactured instruments will be much more affordable. Also, schools purchase instruments and students can borrow them as if they were library books. As long as they keep the instruments in good conditions, they will not be charged extra fees to use the instruments in their classes. So musical instruments being expensive should not be a problem from taking music classes.

이 읽기 지문은 의무 음악 수업이 학교 시스템에 가져오는 몇 가지 흥미로운 문제에 대해 이야기한다. 현실적으로 음악 수업은 학교 안팎에서 수많은 혜택을 제공하기 때문에 읽기 지문에 언급된 문제들은 존재하지 않는다.

읽기 지문은 음악 수업이 학생들의 미래 진로를 준비하는데 무용지물이라고 주장한다. 하지만 음악 수업은 학생들이 다른 수업에서 더 좋은 성적을 내도록 자극하는 데 도움이 된다. 음악 수업은 리듬과 이론을 가르치며, 그것은 수학 수업은 물론 특정 과학 수업에도 적용할 수 있다. 또한 음악 수업의 하이라이트는 학생들이 직접 음악을 만들어 상상력의 한계를 넓히는 것이다. 이것은 학생들이 문학 수업에서 창의적인 에세이를 쓰거나 학교에서 틀에 박히지 않은 프로젝트를 할 때 도움을 줄 수 있다.

음악 수업을 통해 학생들은 다른 분야에서의 성적을 향상시킬 수 있으며, 이것은 그들이 원하는 대학에 입학하고 좋은 직장을 얻을 수 있도록 도와줄 것이다.

음악 수업의 불공평한 성적에 관해서, 학생이 음악 수업을 듣는다는 것은 단순히 그들이 얼마나 음악을 잘 연주하는지에 근거하여 그들의 성적을 낸다는 것을 의미하지는 않는다. 그들의 전반적인 성적은 수업 출석, 참여도, 음악 이론 이해 그리고 보고서에 의해 결정된다. 비록 학생이 음치이거나 악기를 연주할 수 있는 타고난 연주 실력을 가지고 있지 않더라도, 그들의 많은 노력은 수업 통과 점수를 얻게 할 것이다. 그러므로, 학생들이 단지 음악적 재능이 없다고 해서 수업을 듣는 것을 단념해서는 안 된다.

비록 악기는 비싸지만, 이 문제를 극복하는데 도움이 되는 많은 해결책들이 있다. 요즘 바이올린과 플루트는 수요가 많아 대량으로 생산되고 있다. 이 악기들이 대량으로 만들어졌기 때문에 이는 비용 감소로 이어졌다. 학생이 수공예 악기를 원하지 않는 한, 이렇게 제조된 악기들은 훨씬 더 저렴할 것이다. 또한 학교가 악기를 구입하고 학생들은 그것을 도서관의 책처럼 빌릴 수 있다. 그들이 악기를 좋은 상태로 유지하는 한, 교실에서 악기를 사용하기 위한 추가 비용이 들지 않을 것이다. 그러므로 악기가 비싸다는 것이 음악 수업을 듣는 것의 문제가 되어서는 안 된다.

ANSWERS AND SCRIPT

Practice4 Page.52

연습4

유전자 변형 농산물, 즉 GMO는 인간의 필요에 더 잘 맞도록 유전적으로 변형된 농산물 들이다. 대부분의 GMO는 인간이 일상 생활에서 섭취하는 과일, 식물, 가축이다. GMO를 지지하는 사람들은 몇 가지 이유로 GMO가 필요하다고 주장할 것이다.

이런 유전자 변형 식품이 없다면, 인류는 식량 부족에 직면할 것이다.
GMO는 날씨나 계절적 조건 제약 없이 단기간 그리고 1년 내내 재배할 수 있도록 만들어졌다. 예를 들어, 토마토에는 북극 어류에서 발견되는 특정 유전자가 주입되었다. 북극 어류는 어는점 이하의 수온에서 헤엄치기 때문에, 그들의 몸은 부동 화학 물질을 방출하여, 물고기가 추운 환경에서 살아남을 수 있게 한다. 이 부동 유전자는 추운 겨울에도 토마토를 재배할 수 있도록 토마토의 DNA에 주입되었다. 이러한 유전자 변형은 식량이 결코 부족해지지 않도록 한다.

게다가, 유전자 변형 농산물은 수백 년 이상 존재해 왔다. 유전학의 아버지인 그레고르 멘델은 완두콩의 유전자 공급원을 바꿔서 원하는 특성을 만들어 낸 것으로 인정받고 있지만, 인간은 기원전 8000년부터 GMO를 만들어 왔다. 농부들과 목축업자들은 선택적 사육과 교배 작용을 이용하여 원하는 특성을 가진 동식물을 창조하였다.
그 이후로, 어떤 위험한 부작용도 발견되지 않았고 GMO를 섭취하는 사람들도 그로 인한 어떠한 질병이나 원하지 않는 부작용이 나타나지 않았다. 따라서 GMO는 먹어도 안전하며 소비자들이 이를 경계하지 않아도 무방하다.

마지막으로 GMO를 만드는 공학적인 과정을 통해, 과학자는 유전학 분야에서 큰 발전을 이루었다. 유기체의 DNA를 분석함으로써, 과학자들은 유전학의 복잡성을 이해하게 되었고, 그들이 간단한 음식 이외의 영역에서 습득한 것을 적용하는 법을 배웠다. 예를 들어 제약 회사들은 식물과 동물의 특정한 특성을 이용하여 인류를 이롭게 하는 개선된 약을 만들어냈다. 이처럼 GMO 덕분에 과학 분야는 더 진보할 수 있었다.

Practice4 Page.54

Integrated Practice 4
(Male Professor)

The author of the reading passage is wrong in believing that genetically modified organisms, or GMO, are safe. Let me tell you why the three points mentioned in the reading are erroneous.

First, although it seems that GMO provide a solution to food shortage, it is only a temporary solution because of the negative side effect of growing GMO. In order to farm these genetically modified crops, certain pesticides must be used. However, these pesticides only contribute to pesticide-resistant pests, so in a short matter of time, more of these pests will surface and consume the GMO that are growing in the fields. Making matters worse, the new pesticide resistant bugs will consume non-GMO produce and farmers will be left with nothing to farm. Therefore, the answer to food shortage does not lie in genetically modified organisms.

Moreover, GMO do not seem to have any side effects on the surface, but it is wrong to assume that GMO are safe to eat. Scientists now believe that GMO are somewhat related to various types of cancer. In the last 40 years, more cases of cancer have been diagnosed all over the world. It is no coincidence that GMO produce and meat hit the shelves of supermarkets relatively around the same time. Cancer is actually found dormant in every human being. Specific mutations in the DNA or environmental factors cause cancer to appear. It is believed that years of consuming GMO products have mutated our DNA and caused more cancer patients to be diagnosed.

Finally, regarding the issue of scientific achievement through genetically modified organisms, many groups and countries believe that such scientific success should not be brought forth by meddling with Godly affairs. Many people believe that a superior being created each organism for a specific purpose and role in the world. By forcing a change in the organisms, humans are stepping into a realm they should not be in. Religious groups call this a taboo and constantly hold rallies and appeal to court of laws to ban GMO from their country. They believe that any advancement should come from hard work without stepping in the boundaries of gods.

읽기 지문의 저자가 유전자 변형 농산물, 즉 GMO가 안전하다고 믿는 것은 잘못된 것이다. 읽기 지문에 언급된 세 가지 점이 왜 틀렸는지 말해 보려 한다.

첫째, GMO가 식량난에 대한 해결책을 제공하는 것처럼 보이지만, GMO를 재배하는 데서 오는 부정적인 부작용 때문에 그것은 일시적인 해결책에 불과하다. 이러한 유전사 변형 작물을 재배하기 위해서는 반드시 특정 농약을 사용해야 한다. 그러나 이러한 살충제는 오히려 살충제 내성 해충을 만들어 내게 되고, 단기간에 더 많은 해충이 나타나 밭에서 자라고 있는 GMO를 먹어 치우게 된다. 설상가상으로, 새로운 살충세 내성 해충들은 GMO가 아닌 농산물을 먹어 치울 것이고 농부들은 농사를 지을 것이 아무것도 없게 될 것이다. 따라서 식량 부족에 대한 해답은 유전자 변형 농산물에 있지 않다.

더구나 GMO는 겉으로 보기에는 부작용이 없어 보이지만, 그렇다고 해서 GMO를 먹어도 안전하다고 가정하는 것은 잘못되었다. 과학자들은 현재 GMO가 다양한 종류의 암과 어느 정도 관련이 있다고 믿고 있다. 지난 40년 동안 전 세계적으로 더 많은 암이 진단되었다. GMO 생산품과 GMO 고기가 비교적 비슷한 시기에 슈퍼마켓 진열대에 오른 것은 우연이 아니다. 암은 사실 모든 인간에게 잠재되어 있다. DNA의 특정한 돌연변이나 환경적 요인은 암을 유발한다. 수 년간 GMO 제품을 소비한 것이

ANSWERS AND SCRIPT

우리의 DNA를 변이 시켰고 이로 인해 더 많은 환자들이 암 진단을 받게 되었다고 여겨진다.

마지막으로 유전자 조작 농산물을 통한 과학적 성취에 대해 많은 단체와 국가들은 이러한 과학적 성공이 신의 영역을 침범해서는 안 된다고 믿는다. 많은 사람들은 한 초월자가 각각의 유기체가 이 세상에서 특정한 목적과 역할을 갖도록 창조했다고 믿는다. 유기체를 변화시킴으로써, 인간은 그들이 침범해서는 안 되는 영역으로 발을 들여 놓고 있다. 종교 단체들은 이를 금지시키며 끊임없이 집회를 열고 GMO를 자국으로부터 금지시키기 위해 법원에 호소한다. 그들은 신의 영역을 침범하지 않는 선에서 열심히 노력함으로써 진보가 생겨나야 한다고 믿는다.

Practice5 Page.60

연습5

최근, 투표를 위한 전자 투표 기표소의 활용이 널리 퍼지고 있다. 투표를 수합하는 이러한 방식은 몇 가지 장점들을 갖는다.

첫 번째 장점은 수 많은 사람들이 이러한 방식을 통해 투표에 참여할 수 있다는 점이다. 투표는 간단히 화면을 터치하는 것으로 이루어지며, 따라서 유권자들은 기표소에 빠르게 드나들 수 있다. 전자 투표 기표소는 기계이기 때문에, 지치지 않을 것이고, 따라서 하루 종일 쉴 필요가 없을 것이다. 또한, 기표소는 도시의 다른 곳에 위치할 수 있다. 투표가 사람들에 의해서 운영될 때는, 유권자들이 가서 투표를 할 수 있는 장소가 한정되어 있었다. 그러나 전자 기표소는 사람들의 운영이 필요하지 않기 때문에, 동네 슈퍼마켓이나 은행에 위치할 수 있을 것이고, 따라서 사람들은 누구나 언제든지 활용할 수 있을 것이다.

전자 투표 기표소의 두 번째 장점은 정확하게 투표할 수 있다는 점이다. 일부 사람들은 악필이어서, 그들의 표는 때때로 오해의 소지가 있는 것으로 밝혀졌다. 또한 전자 투표 기표소는 사람들의 상호 작용을 필요로 하지 않는다. 투표를 하기 위해 줄을 서 있는 동안, 또는 관리자들을 마주하였을 때, 의견을 주고 받을 수 있고, 따라서 유권자들은 다른 쪽으로 투표하도록 흔들릴 수 있다. 기표소는 베일에 싸여 있고 유권자들이 유일하게 상호 작용 하는 것은 의견을 내지 않는 컴퓨터 화면이므로, 그들은 편견에 치우치지 않은 결정을 할 수 있다.

전자 투표 기표소의 세 번째 장점은 오류가 발생할 확률이 낮다는 것이다. 표를 셀 때, 사람들은 수를 세는 동안 실수하기 쉽다. 그러나, 기계는 표를 전기적으로 세기 때문에 오차가 없다. 때때로 투표 용지에 적힌 질문이나 문구가 혼란스러운 방식으로 적혀 있을 수 있어서, 영어가 모국어가 아닌 사람들이나 나이든 사람들은 어떻게, 무엇을 투표해야 하는지 헷갈릴 수 있다. 그러나, 컴퓨터 화면은 컬러 코드화 되어있고, 선택지들은 단순한 방법으로 보여지기 때문에, 실수를 할 확률이 적다.

Practice5 Page.62

Integrated Practice 5
(Female Professor)
Ok. So the author points out that electronic voting booths offer several advantages over the traditional voting methods. The author could not be more misled. Electronic voting methods actually have some serious problems.

The reading states that more people will have access to voting by using the electronic booths. However, since these voting booths are machines, they are likely to break down and stop the voting process. Unless a mechanic hurries over and fixes the problem, people will be delayed from voting and might not even have a chance to vote if they came the last minute. This actually happened during the recent presidential election. A number of machines manufactured by the same company had deployed machines with a mechanical flaw. On the day of the vote, these machines did not turn on and thousands of voters from that city failed to participate in the presidential vote. What a loss.

Also, electronic voting booths do not bring about accurate votes. Even though there is no human interaction while using the machines, the machines are still strategically placed around the different candidate's territory. There will be banners outside that will elude the uncertain voter, and rallies and chants from across the street will still cause the voter to be hesitant in the vote that they put in. Like a soccer fan trying to root for his home team while being mixed in the opponent's crowd, he will be swayed from his actions and may end up rooting against his own team.

Finally, electronic voting booths can make errors in counting because they can be hacked. All machines have the probability of being hacked if they are connected to a network. Since the electronic votes are counted in real time, someone clever enough could hack into the voting system and with a few algorithms, can change the number of votes to the favoring side. This is why even amongst the most technologically developed countries around the world, important votes are written on paper and given to the mediator to be counted while a second mediator confirms the vote. In many of the judicial systems, the jury passes judgement on the victim by using paper votes to deliver the verdict to the judge.

ANSWERS AND SCRIPT

저자는 전자 투표 기표소가 기존의 전통적인 투표 방식에 비해 몇 가지 유리한 점이 있다고 말하고 있다. 저자의 의견은 잘못된 점이 많다. 전자 투표 방식은 사실 몇 가지 치명적인 문제점들을 가지고 있다. 글에서는 더 많은 사람들이 전자 기표소를 활용함에 따라 더 투표하기 쉬울 것이라고 언급하고 있다. 그러나 이러한 기표소들은 기계이기 때문에, 고장 나거나 투표 과정이 중단되는 경향이 있다. 정비사가 서둘러서 문제를 수리하지 않는 한, 사람들은 투표가 지연될 것이며, 만약 마지막 몇 분 전에 도착했다면, 그들은 투표를 할 기회를 잃을 수도 있다. 사실 이러한 일은 최근의 대선에서 발생했었다. 동일한 회사에서 제조된 많은 기계들이 기계적인 결함을 지닌 채 배치되었다. 투표일에 이 기계들은 켜지지 않았고, 그 도시의 유권자 수 천명은 대선에 참여하지 못했다. 얼마나 큰 손해인가.

또한 전자 투표 기표소는 정확한 투표를 하지 못하게 한다. 이 기계를 사용하는 동안, 사람들과의 상호작용이 없다 하여도, 이 기계들은 전략적으로 다른 후보자의 영역 근처에 놓여질 수 있다. 확실한 유권자로 만들기 위한 현수막이 걸려 있을 것이고, 맞은편에서 들려오는 집회와 구호는 유권자들이 자신이 하려 했던 투표를 하는데 있어 여전히 주저함을 유발시킬 수 있을 것이다. 상대 관중들 사이에 뒤섞여 자신의 홈 팀을 응원하려는 축구 팬들처럼 그의 행동들은 흔들릴 것이며, 결국 자신의 팀을 등지고 상대를 응원하게 될 것이다.

마지막으로, 전자 투표 기표소는 해킹될 수 있기 때문에 표를 세는데 있어 오류가 생길 수 있다. 모든 기계들이 네트워크에 연결되어 있다면, 해킹될 수 있는 가능성을 가지고 있다. 전자 투표는 실시간으로 개표되기 때문에, 일부 유능한 이들은 몇 개의 알고리즘 만으로 투표 시스템을 충분히 해킹할 수 있고, 그들이 선호하는 측으로 득표수를 바꿀 수 있다. 이러한 이유로 세계에서 가장 기술적으로 발달된 나라들에서도 중요한 투표는 종이가 쓰이며, 두 번째 검표자가 투표를 확인하는 동안 이를 세기 위한 검표자가 있다. 많은 사법 제도에서, 배심원들은 평결문을 판사에게 전달하기 위해 종이 투표를 활용하여, 피해자에 대한 판결을 내린다.

Chapter03
Academic Discussion Essay Lesson

Page.70

학술 토론의 목적은 온라인 수업 토론에서 주어진 주제에 대한 당신의 의견을 진술하고 근거를 제시하는 것이다. 훌륭한 답변에는 당신의 관점을 뒷받침하는 적절한 이유, 예시 및 세부사항이 포함되어야 한다.

교수는 강의를 하는 중이다.
교수의 질문에 답하는 글을 쓰시오.

당신의 답변에서는 아래의 내용이 수행되어야 한다.
- 당신의 의견을 표현하고 근거를 제시한다.
- 토론에 기여한다.

유효한 답변에는 최소 100개의 단어가 포함된다.
주어지는 시간은 10분이다.

교수
온라인 수업 토론, 교수님의 질문.
학생 A
학생 의견
학생 B
학생 의견

수험생에게는 학술 토론 에세이를 쓸 수 있는 10분의 시간이 주어진다. 문제가 제시되자마자, 체계적이고 논리적인 에세이가 나올 수 있도록 브레인스토밍과 개요를 떠올리는 것이 중요하다.

Page.71~73

예시 질문
교수는 사회학 수업을 하고 있다. 교수의 질문에 답하는 글을 쓰시오.

당신은 답변에서 다음을 수행해야 한다.
- 자신의 의견을 표현하고 근거를 제시한다.
- 토론에 기여한다

유효한 응답에는 최소 100개의 단어가 포함된다.
주어지는 시간은 10분이다.

존스 박사
어떤 사람이 범죄를 저질렀을 때, 그들은 그 행위의 심각성에 따라 처벌을 받습니다. 그럼에도 불구하고, 대부분의 범죄자들은 정해진 기간 동안 감옥에 수감됩니다. 수감되는 사람들의 수가 매년 증가하고 있기 때문에, 어떤 사람들은 이것이 범죄를 해결하는 가장 좋은 방법이라고 믿곤 하죠. 어떤 사람들은 사회 봉사가 더 낫다고 생각합니다. 만약 여러분이 처벌 방법을 선택한다면, 어떤 방법이 가장 좋다고 생각하십니까? 그리고 그 이유는 무엇이죠?

미셸
한 사람이 감옥에서 복역함으로써 그들의 범죄에 대한 책임을 지는 것은 당연합니다. 감금된 채 시간을 보내는 동안, 그들은 자신의 실수를 반성하고 더 나은 시민이 될 수 있는 방법을 생각하는 시간을 가질 것입니다. 여전히, 일부 범죄자들은 변화를 거부할 것이고 사회에 위협이 될 것입니다. 그래서 그들이 다시는 예전과 같이 악랄한 행위를 저지르지 못하도록 가두는 것이 최선일 것입니다.

데이빗
저는 범죄자들을 처벌하는 가장 좋은 방법이 그들을 감옥에 보내는 것이라는 미셸의 의견에 동의하지 않습니다. 사회봉사는 사실상 위법 행위를 한 사람들을 처벌하는 가장 좋은 방법입니다. 범죄자들은 자신의 범죄를 사리사욕을 위해 수행했기 때문에, 그들은 그들의 범죄에 대해 공동체를 위해 봉사하는 것이 가장 좋습니다. 그러므로, 저는 범죄자들이 사회봉사를 함으로써 처벌받아야 한다고 생각합니다.

주관적인가 객관적인가?
학문적인 토론은 수험생의 의견을 묻는 것이기는 하지만, 주관적인 에세이보다는 객관적인 에세이를 쓰는 것이 실제로 유익하다는 점에 유의해야 한다.

브레인스토밍 및 개요:
앞서 언급했듯 객관적인 에세이를 쓰기 위해서는 자신의 취향이나 의견보다 자신의 사유가 더 중요하다. 수험생들은 에세이를 타이핑하기 전에 아이디어를 브레인스토밍하는 데 약 1분을 할애해야 한다. 다음은 수험생들이 에세이에 사용할 수 있는 가장 일반적인 이유 중 몇 가지이다.

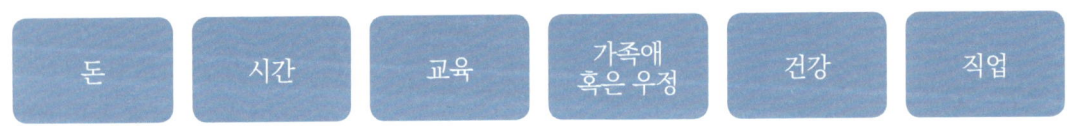

추가 노트

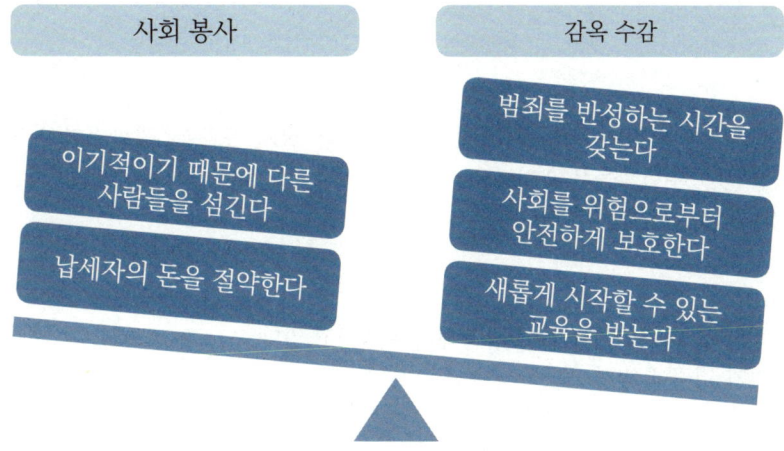

보다시피, 범죄자들을 감옥에 보냄으로써 처벌해야 할 이유가 더 많다.
또한 다른 학생들이 언급한 이유를 선택할 수 있다. 당신은 그들이 제시한 이유로 에세이를 쓰거나 새로운 이유로 당신이 지지하는 것을 선택할 수 있다. 하지만 이미 언급된 아이디어만 다시 사용해서는 안 되며 토론에 자신의 의견을 추가해야 한다. 중요한 점은 에세이에 얼마나 다양한 논리와 설명을 쓸 수 있는가이다.

예를 들어, 여러분은 감옥 생활이 개인들이 과거의 실수를 반성할 수 있게 해준다는 미셸의 말에 동의할지도 모른다. 그러나 이 관점에 자신의 아이디어를 추가해야 한다. 예를 들어, 여러분은 개인이 명상하고 일기를 쓸 수 있다고 주장할 수 있다. 이것은 그들이 생각을 정리하고 심지어 그들이 감옥에서 하는 치료 시간 동안 그 생각을 상기하는 것을 도울 것이다. 이것은 당신의 아이디어를 소개하는 동안 미셸의 관점에 대한 추가적인 지지가 될 것이다.

학술 토론 조직명:

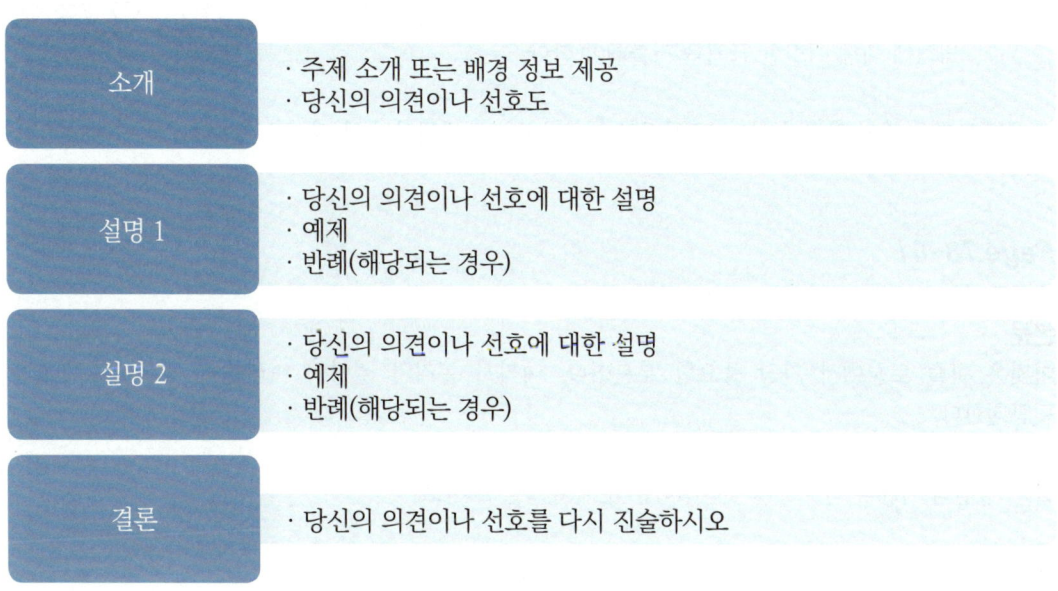

Answers and Script

ANSWERS AND SCRIPT

Page.76~77

소개
도입부 문장은 주제와 작가의 의견을 소개한다. 주의력 잡기 도구는 일반적인 문장으로 서론을 시작하는 데 사용된다. 수험생들은 흥미로운 사실을 쓰거나, 최근 뉴스를 인용하거나, 유명한 인용문을 사용하거나, 명백한 것을 말할 수 있다.

흥미로운 사실
전 세계적으로 천만 명 이상의 사람들이 감옥에서 복역하고 있다.
수감자의 약 20%가 미국에 있다.

유명한 인용문
알버트 아인슈타인은 "다른 사람을 위해 산 삶은 가치 있는 삶이다"라고 말한 적이 있다. 이것은 한 사람의 삶이 지역사회에 봉사함으로써 어떻게 충족되는지 보여준다.

토론 주제
그 교수는 범죄 행위를 한 사람들에 대한 적절한 처벌에 대해 주장한다.

에세이의 서론 부분의 마지막 문장은 교수의 질문에 대한 작가의 의견이나 선호를 언급해야 한다.

좋은 점: 적절한 처벌을 내리는 것과 관련하여, 범죄자들을 감옥에 보내는 것이 더 나은 해결책이다.

때때로, 작가들은 새로운 해결책을 모두 언급하는 것을 선택할 수도 있다. 기억하라, 교수는 특별히 교도소나 사회봉사 중 하나를 선택하라고 했다. 글쓴이는 토론에서 교수가 쓰는 선택지 중에서 선택해야 한다. 학생들이 언급한 이유 외에 새로운 이유를 쓰는 것과 혼동해서는 안 된다.

나쁜 점: 나는 범죄자들이 금전적인 수단으로 처벌받아야 한다고 생각한다. 그들은 그들이 저지른 범죄에 대해 적절한 금액을 지불해야 한다.

도입부 문장은 길지 않아야 한다. 구체적인 아이디어를 소개해서는 안 되며 2분 이내에 작성해야 한다.

Page.78~81

본문
이것은 학술 토론에서 가장 중요한 부분이다. 여기서 논리와 설명이 여러분의 의견이나 선호를 뒷받침한다.

설명: 당신의 이유나 선호도를 뒷받침하는 두세 문장을 쓰시오.

예시: 개인적인 경험, 뉴스, 역사, 역사적 인물 또는 통계에 대해 설명한다.

반대예시: 자신의 의견이나 참고문헌과 비교하여 반대 의견이나 선택지의 약점을 보여주는 예문이나 진술.

설명: 감옥에서 시간을 보내는 것은 사람들로 하여금 그들의 과거의 실수를 반성하게 할 것이다. 아이들이 잘못된 행동을 했을 때 무엇을 잘못했는지 생각할 수 있는 시간이 주어지듯이, 범죄자들은 감옥에서 시간이 주어져야 한다. 감옥에 있는 동안, 흉악범들은 그들의 범죄에 대해 생각할 수 있고 아마도 그들의 범죄에 대해 속죄할 수 있을 것이다.

예: 오늘날, 수감자들은 그들의 생각을 기록하기 위해 일기를 쓴다. 그리고 나서, 그들은 치료나 집단상담에서 다른 사람들과 그들의 생각을 공유한다.

반대 예: 하지만, 범죄자들은 사회봉사를 할 때 쓰레기를 줍거나 육체노동을 하느라 너무 바쁠 것이기 때문에 그들의 범죄를 뉘우칠 기회가 없을 것이다.

설명을 작성하면서 한 가지 주의할 점은 일관성이다. 일관성은 에세이에서 제시된 아이디어의 흐름을 말한다. 문장들은 같은 생각과 설명을 공유함으로써 서로 연결되어야 한다.

나쁜 일관성: 감옥에서 시간을 보내는 것은 개인들로 하여금 그들의 과거의 실수에 대해 반성하게 할 것이다. 신체가 육체노동을 하느라 바쁠 것이기 때문에 사회봉사는 중재를 허용하지 않는다.
　　이 단락의 일관성은 실제로 좋지 않다. 왜냐하면 설명은 감옥에서 시간을 보내는 것이 개인들이 그들의 과거의 실수를 반성할 수 있게 해줄 것이라고 말하는 것으로 시작하기 때문이다. 그래서 다음 문장은 왜 개인들이 감옥에서 명상을 할 수 있는지 또는 어떻게 하는지에 대해 논의해야 하지만, 대신 사회봉사가 반성을 허용하지 않는 이유를 언급한다. 비록 이 생각의 흐름이 보통 사람들에게는 잘못 들리지 않을 지라도, 문장은 이전에 쓰여진 것과 연결되어야 한다.

좋은 일관성: 감옥에서 시간을 보내는 것은 개인들이 그들의 과거의 실수에 대해 반성할 수 있게 해줄 것이다. 아이들이 잘못된 행동을 했을 때 무엇을 잘못했는지 생각할 수 있는 시간이 주어지듯이, 범죄자들은 감옥에서 시간이 주어져야 한다.
　　보다시피, 그 문장들은 모두 연결되어 있다. 왜냐하면 그 문장들은 범죄자들이 그들이 무엇을 잘못했는지 생각하기 위해 왜 감옥에 가야 하는지에 대해 논의하기 때문이나.

예문이라도 앞에 쓴 문장과 일관성이 있어야 한다.

잘못된 일관성: 감옥에 있는 동안, 흉악범들은 과거를 되돌아볼 수 있을 것이다. 그들의 범죄에 대해 그리고 아마도 그들의 범죄에 대해 속죄할 것이다. 오렌지색 점프슈트를 입고 고속도로를 따라 쓰레기를 줍는 동안, 범죄자들은 들어오는 차들에 치이지 않고 쓰레기를 줍는 데 집중해야 한다.
　　이 예시는 설명과 관련이 없으며 중죄인이 감옥에 있는 동안 자신의 범죄를 되돌아볼 수 있는 것에 대해 논의하지 않는다. 여기서 예는 설명과 일관성이 없다.

양호한 일관성: 감옥에 있는 동안, 흉악범들은 그들의 범죄에 대해 생각할 수 있고 아마도 그들의 범죄에 대해 속죄할 수 있을 것이다.

오늘날, 수감자들은 그들의 생각을 기록하기 위해 일기를 쓴다. 그리고 나서, 그들은 치료나 집단 상담에서 다른 사람들과 그들의 생각을 공유한다.

그 예시와 그 전의 설명은 같은 생각으로 연결되어 있는데, 그것은 흉악범들이 자신의 죄를 뉘우칠 수 있다는 것이다.

Page.82

결론:
학술 토론 에세이의 마지막 문장이다. 여기에 새로운 정보를 명시해서는 안 되며, 작성자의 의견이나 선호도를 다시 진술한다.

그러므로, 범죄자들에 대한 올바른 처벌을 통과시키는 것에 있어서, 그들을 감옥에 보내는 것이 그들에게 사회봉사를 시키는 것보다 더 나은 해결책이다.

일부 수험생은 결론 문장을 쓸 시간이 충분하지 않을 수도 있다. 특히 마지막 문장이 예문이라면 결론 없이 에세이를 끝내는 것이 조금 어색할 수도 있다. 루브릭은 결론 문장이 필요하다고 명시하지 않지만, 수험생들이 그것을 쓸 시간이 있다면, 그들은 분명히 그것을 포함해야 한다.

편집:
에세이를 한 번쯤 교정해 보기 전까지는 에세이가 완성되지 않는다. 믿거나 말거나, 심지어 최고의 작가들도 시간이 다 가기 전에 에세이를 끝내기 위해 서두르기 때문에 에세이를 쓸 시간이 정해져 있을 때 실수를 하기 쉽다.

단순한 실수는 다음과 같다:
- 철자 오류
- 문법적 오류: 주어 동사 일치 및 대명사 일치
- 대문자화 오류
- 구두점 오류

이것들은 이 에세이를 쓰는 데 주어진 10분에서 마지막 1분이나 1초 안에 수정되어야 하는 식별하기 쉬운 실수들이다.

Page.83~84

샘플 에세이 1:
전 세계적으로 천만 명 이상의 사람들이 감옥에서 복역하고 있다. 수감자의 약 20%가 미국에 있다. 적절한 처벌과 관련하여, 범죄자들을 감옥에 보내는 것이 더 나은 해결책이다. 감옥에서 시간을 보내는 것은 개인들이 과거의 실수를 반성할 수 있게 해줄 것이다. 아이들이 잘못된 행동을 했을 때 무엇을 잘못했는지 생각할 수 있는 시간이 주어지듯이, 범죄자들은 감옥에서 시간이 주어져야 한다. 감옥에 있는 동안, 흉악범들은 그들의 범죄에 대해 생각할 수 있고 아마도 그들의 범죄에 대해 속죄할 수 있을 것이다. 오늘날, 수감자들은 그들의 생각을 기록하기 위해 일기를 쓴다. 그리고 나서, 그들은 치료나 집단 상담에서 다른 사람들과 그들의 생각을 공유한다. 하지만, 범죄자들은 사회봉사를 할 때 쓰레기를 줍거나 육체노동을 하느라 너무 바쁠 것이기 때문에 그들의 범죄를 뉘우칠 기회가 없을 것이다. 그러므로, 범죄자들에 대한 올바른 처벌을 통과시키는 것에 있어서, 그들을 감옥에 보내는 것이 그들에게 사회봉사를 시키는 것보다 더 나은 해결책이다.
181개의 단어.

점수: 5
이 에세이는 완전히 성공적인 답변이다. 작가는 범죄자들을 처벌하는 가장 좋은 방법으로 징역형을 선택한다. 그런 다음 글쓴이는 어떻게 감옥 생활이 흉악범들이 그들의 범죄에 대해 숙고하고 그들이 가지고 있는 것을 회개하도록 허락할 것인지에 대한 설명을 제공한다. 글쓴이는 계속해서 지역사회 봉사는 이러한 명상 시간이 부족하기 때문에, 그것은 처벌로서 적절하지 않다고 지적한다. 전반적으로, 이 에세이는 작가의 선호를 뒷받침하기 위해 일관성 있는 설명과 세부 사항을 제공하고 교수의 온라인 토론에 관련된 기여를 제공한다. 작가는 또한 몇몇 복잡한 문장 구조와 적절한 어휘를 사용한다.

샘플 에세이 2:
범죄자들은 그들의 범죄에 대한 벌로 쓰레기를 줍고 다른 사회봉사를 해야 한다. 이 사람들은 매우 이기적이었고 자신들의 이익을 위해 범죄를 저질렀다. 예를 들어, 그들은 부자가 되기 위해 은행을 털었을 수도 있다. 아니면 그들은 차가 없어서 차를 훔쳤을 수도 있다. 범죄자들은 자신의 이익을 위해 행동했기 때문에, 그들의 처벌은 다른 사람들을 위해 봉사하는 것이어야 한다. 쓰레기를 줍는 것과 같은 사회 봉사를 함으로써, 그들은 다른 사람들을 섬기는 것의 중요성을 배우고 이기적이지 않을 것이다. 그러므로, 범죄자들을 처벌하는 가장 좋은 방법은 그들을 감옥에 보내는 대신 사회봉사이다.
100단어.

점수: 3
이 에세이는 부분적으로 성공적인 답변이다. 작가는 범죄자를 처벌하는 가장 좋은 방법으로 사회봉사를 선택한다. 그리고 나서 작가는 왜 사회봉사가 범죄자들에게 공평한 처벌인지에 대한 설명을 제공한다. 하지만, 그것은 왜 다른 사람들을 섬기는 것이 적절한 처벌인지 더 자세히 설명하지 못한다. 글쓴이는 감옥에 가는 것이 다른 사람을 섬기는 행위가 되지 않을 것이라고 언급할 수도 있었으므로, 이 이기적인 사람들에게는 적절한 처벌이 아니다. 문장 구조에는 약간의 다양성이 있지만, 어휘의 사용은 제한적이다. 예를 들어, 글쓴이는 범죄를 저지른 사람들을 묘사하기 위해 "범죄자"라는 단어만 사용한다. 또한 단어 수는 정확히 100개의 단어로 학술 토론 에세이의 최소 단어 수이다.

학술 토론 에세이의 공식 단어 수는 100단어이다. 통합 단어 수와 마찬가지로 공식 단어 수는 최소이며 논리적인 에세이를 쓰기에 충분하지 않을 것이다. 200단어짜리 에세이도 충분하지만, 단어가 많을수록 더 많은 실수가 일어날 수 있다는 것을 명심하라.

당신은 왜 학술 토론 에세이에서 낮은 점수를 받을까?

1) 에세이 질문에 대한 오해:
   때때로, 수험생들은 문제를 급하게 읽거나 잘못 해석할 수도 있다. 질문을 잘 읽고 질문에 완전히 답해야 한다. 질문에 "아니오"와 같은 간단한 단어는 완전히 다른 에세이를 만들 수 있다.

2) 논리 없음:
   학술 토론 에세이는 이야기책이 되어서는 안 된다. 다시 말해서, 예제가 에세이 전체를 차지해서는 안 된다. 논리적인 설명은 몇 개의 문장만 사용하는 예제로 뒷받침되어야 한다.

3) 내용:
   대부분의 포인트는 이 영역에서 차감된다. 당신의 의견에 대한 설명은 타당해야 하고, 에세이에 쓰인 아이디어들의 일관성이 일치해야 하며, 에세이의 구성이 명확해야 한다.

4) 문법 및 철자 오류:
   문법과 철자를 틀리면 점수가 차감된다. 그러니 마지막 순간에 에세이를 꼭 수정하시오.

5) 미완성 에세이:
   학술 토론은 단지 10분 동안만 쓸 수 있다. 에세이 쓰기를 마치기 위해 틈틈이 시간을 확인하라.

Chapter04
Academic Discussion Essay Practices

Page.88~92

연습1
교수는 환경 과학 수업을 하고 있는 중이다. 교수의 질문에 답하는 글을 쓰시오.

당신의 답변에서 다음을 수행해야 한다:
- 당신의 의견을 표현하고 지지한다
- 토론에 기여한다

유효한 응답에는 최소 100개의 단어가 포함된다. 당신은 그것을 쓸 시간이 10분 있을 것이다.

밀러 교수
지구 온난화가 전 세계의 문명을 위협하고 있는 가운데, 지구의 지속적인 온도 상승과 관련된 문제들에 대처하는 것이 필수적이 되었습니다. 과학자들과 환경 운동가들은 지구 온난화와 싸우는 것을 돕기 위한 여러 가지 해결책을 제안했습니다. 지구 온난화를 줄이는 가장 효과적인 방법은 무엇이라고 생각하십니까? 그 이유는?

새라
저는 휘발유 자동차의 사용을 줄이는 것이 지구 온난화와 관련된 문제들을 완화하는 데 도움이 될 것이라고 말하고 싶습니다. 가솔린 자동차와 버스의 탄소 배출로 인해 기온이 상승하고 있습니다. 사람들이 대안을 사용하는 경우 전기자동차와 같은 운송수단, 탄소배출량이 감소할 것이고 지구온난화도 뒤따를 것입니다.

제이크
저는 학교가 지구 온난화의 원인과 영향에 대해 학생들을 교육하는 일을 더 잘 할 수 있다고 생각합니다. 제 친구들 대부분은 사실 지구 온난화의 원인과 그것과 관련된 위험에 대해 알지 못합니다. 만약 교수들이 지구 온난회에 대한 정보를 학생들에게 전달한다면, 젊은 세대들은 그들의 생활 방식을 바꿀 수 있을 것이고, 이것은 궁극적으로 미래의 지구 기온에 영향을 미칠 것입니다.

샘플 에세이 1
지구 온난화와 싸우는 많은 다른 방법들이 있다. 나는 지구 온난화를 해결하는 가장 좋은 방법은 친환경 자동차를 이용하는 것이라고 생각한다. 나는 탄소 배출이 지구 온난화의 근본 원인 중 하나라는 사라의 말에 동의한다. 나는 수소 연료와 같은 대체 연료를 사용하는 것은 탄소 배출량을 0으로 만들기 때문에 지구 온난화에 기여하지 않는다고 덧붙이고 싶다. Jake는 학생들을 교육하는 해결책을 제안했지만, 이것은 효과적인 해결책이 아니다. 나는 초등학교 때 지구 온난화에 대해 배웠지만, 솔직히 지구 온난화의 위험에 대해 신경을 쓰기에는 너무 어렸다. 친구들과 노느라 바빴다. 그러므로, 지구 온난화를 해결하는 가장 좋은 방법은 비 휘발유 자동차를 사용하는 것이다.
131단어

샘플 에세이 2
사실 오존층에는 해로운 햇빛이 대기로 들어오게 하는 구멍이 있다. 이것은 지구 온난화의 원인 중 하나이다. 지구 온난화를 줄이기 위한 가장 실용적인 해결책은 HCFC나 CFC를 사용하는 제품을 사용하지 않는 것이다. 추진제. 이 화학물질들은 오존층을 약화시키는 원인이 된다. 이러한 화학 물질을 사용하는 제품의 사용을 중단함으로써 오존층이 복원될 것이다. HCFC 또는 CFC를 사용하는 제품 중에는 에어컨 장치, 냉장고, 헤어 스프레이가 포함되어 있다. 사람들은 더 안전한 화학 물질을 사용하고 수성 헤어 스프레이로 머리를 스타일링하는 가전제품을 사용할 수 있다. 그러면, 지구 온난화는 확실히 멈출 것이다.
115단어

Page.94~98

연습2
교수는 사회 과목을 가르치는 중이다.
교수의 질문에 답하는 글을 쓰시오.

당신의 답변에서 다음을 수행해야 한다:
- 당신의 의견을 표현하고 지지한다
- 토론에 기여한다

유효한 응답에는 최소 100개의 단어가 포함된다.
당신에게는 그것을 쓸 시간이 10분 주어질 것이다.

존슨 박사
저는 소셜 미디어가 사회에 미치는 영향에 대해 논의하고 싶습니다. 소셜 미디어의 초기 단계는 단순한 문자 메시지 게시로 시작되었습니다. 그리고 나서 갑자기, 사람들은 세상에 그들이 무엇을 하고 있는지 보여주기 위해 사진과 비디오를 올릴 수 있었습니다. 물론, 그러한 발전은 장단점이 있습니다. 한 편에서는, 사람들은 소셜 미디어가 전세계의 사람들을 연결해주는 것에 대해 박수를 보냅니다. 반면에, 비평가들은 소셜 미디어가 잘못된 정보를 퍼뜨리고 사이버 폭력을 유발한다고 주장합니다. 소셜 미디어에 대한 당신의 입장은 무엇입니까? 이것은 유익한 도구인가요, 아니면 해를 끼치는 무언가인가요?

안드레아
소셜 미디어는 의심할 여지없이 사회에 이익이 됩니다. 페이스북과 인스타그램과 같은 소셜 미디어 플랫폼을 통해 오랫동안 보지 못했던 옛 친구들과 연결될 수 있었습니다. 소셜 미디어는 또한 사람들이 서로 멀리 떨어져 있을 때 연결을 유지하도록 도와줍니다. 저는 한국에 사촌이 있는데, 그 사촌은

저입니다. 소셜 미디어 플랫폼 덕분에 여기 미국에서 연락을 유지할 수 있습니다.

윌리엄
소셜 미디어는 득보다 실이 더 많습니다. 너무 많은 사람들이 소셜 미디어 플랫폼에 중독되어 있어서 그들은 하루의 반 이상을 무작위로 사람들의 프로필을 보거나 매초마다 자신의 사진을 게시하는 데 보냅니다. 사람들은 그들 앞에서 가족과 친구들과 어울리는 대신에 온라인 친구들을 보고 그들이 무엇을 하고 있는지를 보느라 너무 바쁩니다.

샘플 에세이 1
그 교수는 소셜 미디어가 사회에 이로운지 해로운지에 대해 토론한다. 나는 소셜 미디어가 득보다 실이 많다고 생각한다. 나는 사람들이 소셜 미디어에 너무 많은 시간을 쓴다는 윌리엄의 말에 동의한다. 소셜 미디어 사용자들은 직접 앞에 있는 사람들과 양질의 시간을 보내는 대신 스마트폰이나 컴퓨터로 시간을 보내는 것을 선호한다. 이 때문에, 우리 사회에서 진정한 관계의 중요성은 악화되고 있다. 내가 커피숍에 들어갈 때마다, 나는 커플들과 친구들이 그들 앞에 있는 사람과 이야기하는 대신 그들의 전화기를 응시하고 소셜 미디어 플랫폼을 보는 것을 보곤 했다. 모든 관계에서 가장 중요한 것은 대화를 하는 것이기 때문에 이것은 가족과 친구들을 갈라놓았다. 대신, 소셜 미디어는 대화가 일어나는 것을 금지하고 디지털 화면에 사람들의 시선을 집중시켰다. 따라서, 소셜 미디어는 진정한 관계를 빼앗아 감으로써 사회에 해를 끼친다.
151단어

샘플 에세이 2
페이스북은 최근 151개의 단어들을 그들의 플랫폼에 비디오 채팅 시스템을 설치했다. 그래서 이제 사용자들은 사랑하는 사람들의 얼굴을 볼 수 있다. 이처럼 소셜 미디어는 사회의 필수적인 부분이며 사람들은 소셜 미디어가 제공하는 이점을 받아들여야 한다. 우선, 소셜 미디어는 사람들이 자신의 상태나 사진을 게시하여 다른 사람들이 자신이 어떻게 지내는지 알 수 있도록 한다.
한국에는 "무소식이 희소식이다"라는 속담이 있다. 그래서 여러분의 가족이나 친구들이 여러분에게 전화를 하지 않을 수도 있지만, 소셜 미디어에서 그들의 상태나 사진을 보는 것만으로도 여러분은 그들이 잘 지내고 있다는 것을 알게 될 것이다. 게다가, 소셜 미디어는 새로운 관계가 형성되는 것을 가능하게 한다. 종종, 사람들은 공부하거나 일하느라 너무 바빠서 밖에 나가서 새로운 친구들을 사귀기 위한 노력을 할 시간이 없다. 하지만, 소셜 미디어는 그들의 취미와 관심사에 근거하여 사람들을 연결시켜 사용자들이 새로운 친구들을 사귀는데 그렇게 많은 노력을 들이지 않아도 되도록 한다. 그러므로, 소셜 미디어는 우리 사회에 유익하다.
173단어

Page.100~104

연습3
교수는 교육에 대한 수업을 하는 중이다.
교수의 질문에 답하는 글을 쓰시오.

ANSWERS AND SCRIPT

당신의 답변에서 다음을 수행해야 한다:
- 당신의 의견을 표현하고 지지한다
- 토론에 기여한다

유효한 응답에는 최소 100개의 단어가 포함된다.
당신은 그것을 쓸 시간이 10분 있을 것이다.

킴벌리 교수
오늘 수업시간에, 저는 학생들을 평가하는 가장 좋은 방법에 대해 이야기하려고 합니다.
이제, 여러분 대부분은 정기적으로 보는 시험에 기초하여 점수를 받습니다. 물론, 시험을 보는 것에 대한 대안들이 있습니다. 제 동료들 중 몇몇은 학생들의 수업 참여도를 기준으로 점수를 매깁니다. 다른 사람들은 제출한 숙제에 근거하여 점수를 줍니다. 여전히, 어떤 사람들은 학생들을 수업 출석에만 점수를 매깁니다. 학생들의 점수를 매기는 다른 많은 방법들이 있습니다. 당신은 어떤 채점 방법이 가장 효과적이라고 생각합니까? 그리고 그 이유는 뭐죠?

마크
저는 학생들의 점수를 매기는 가장 좋은 방법은 숙제라고 생각합니다. 저와 같은 몇몇 학생들은 시험을 준비하기 위해 많은 정보를 암기하는데 어려움을 겪습니다. 하지만, 숙제는 학생들이 그 주에 전달된 수업을 이해했는지 확인하기 위해 확인합니다. 저는 학생들이 그 주에 가르쳤던 개념을 이해하기만 한다면 숙제에 기반한 채점으로 충분해야 한다고 생각합니다.

제시카
학생들의 점수를 매기는 가장 좋은 방법은 대부분의 교수들이 사용하는 시험입니다. 중간고사나 기말고사는 학생들이 수업에 대한 포괄적인 이해를 확실히 하는 좋은 방법입니다. 누구나 그 날의 수업을 기억할 수 있지만, 모든 사람이 몇 주 동안의 정보를 기억하고 이해할 수 있는 것은 아닙니다. 그러므로, 학생들이 시험을 보게 하는 것은 그들의 지능을 표시하는 확실한 방법입니다.

샘플 에세이 1
교육의 목표는 학생들이 배우는 것이다. 만약 학생들이 성적에 부담을 느낀다면, 그들은 귀중한 교훈을 배울 기회를 잃게 될 것이다. 이 부담을 줄이기 위해 학생들의 점수를 매기는 효과적인 방법은 참여에 기초한 점수를 매기는 것이다. 학생들은 참여하면서 교수님께 이해를 표시하는 동시에 수업에 대한 호기심을 보여주고 있다. 결국, 어떤 주제에 호기심을 갖는 것은 지식의 습득이다. 그래서 학생들이 참여도에 따라 점수를 매길 때, 그들은 스트레스를 덜 받을 뿐만 아니라 호기심을 갖기 위한 열린 마음을 가질 것이다. 다른 채점 방법들은 학생들이 참여하고 탐구적인 마음을 보이는 것을 방해할 것이기 때문에, 그러한 방법들은 학생들을 채점하는 것을 금지해야 한다.
125단어

샘플 에세이 2
교수는 학생들의 점수를 매기는 몇 가지 방법을 언급하지만, 저는 학생들의 점수를 매기는 가장 좋은 방법은 시험을 통해서라고 생각한다. 저는 시험이 학생들의 수업에 대한 포괄적인 이해를 확인하는 좋은 방법이라는 점에서 제시카의 의견에 동의한다. 나는 또한 시험에 기초한 성적은 학생들이 그들의 미래 직업에서 무엇을 평가받을 것인지를 반영한다는 것을 지적하고 싶다. 예를 들어, 회사 사무실에서 일할 때, 직원들은 그들이 소개한 작품을 기준으로 평가될 것이다. 이 작업들은 그들의 업무 경험과 축적된 지식을 바탕으로 한 포괄적인 과제가 될 것이다. 숙제가 학생들의 점수를 매기는 가장 좋은 방법이라는 마크의 의견은 그들의 그 과목에 대한 포괄적인 이해를 찾는 것에 미치지 못한다. 그러므로, 학생들이 미래의 진로와 그들이 어떻게 평가될 것인지를 준비하기 위해서, 시험에 근거하여 그들을 채점하는 것이 가장 효과적인 방법이다.
152단어

Page.106~110

연습 4
교수는 정치학 수업을 하는 중이다.
교수의 질문에 답하는 글을 쓰시오.

당신의 답변에서 다음을 수행해야 한다:
- 당신의 의견을 표현하고 지지한다
- 토론에 기여한다

유효한 응답에는 최소 100개의 단어가 포함된다.
당신은 그것을 쓸 시간이 10분 있을 것이다.

모랄레스 박사
정부가 담배와 술과 같은 건강에 좋지 않은 제품에 더 높은 세금을 부과해야 하는지에 대해 논의해 봅시다. 이러한 제품에 더 높은 세금을 부과하도록 함으로써, 사람들은 제품을 소비하는 것을 단념하고 제품과 관련된 건강 문제를 줄일 것입니다. 그럼에도 불구하고, 일부 사람들은 높은 세금을 부과하는 것이 시민들이 이 제품들을 복용함으로써 얻는 특정한 즐거움을 빼앗기 때문에 불공평하다고 주장합니다. 이것에 대해 어떻게 생각합니까? 그리고 이유는 무엇입니까?

마리아
정부는 담배와 술과 같은 상품에 더 높은 세금을 부과할 권리가 없습니다. 정부가 국민들이 건강하게 살 수 있도록 이 제품들에 탐닉하지 않도록 돕고 싶은 마음은 이해하지만, 국민들에게 건상한 생활을 강요하는 것은 국가의 역할이 아닙니다. 사람들이 그들의 몸에 무엇을 하는지는 사람들이 결정해야 합니다.

리차드
정부는 국민의 복시를 위해 존재하기 때문에, 몸에 좋지 않은 제품에 더 높은 세금을 부과할 권리가 있습니다. 정부는 부모와 같습니다. 만약 부모가 그녀의 아이들이 그들의 몸에 해로운 제품을 먹는 것을 본다면, 그들은 무슨 수를 써서라도 그들을 막아야 합니다. 더 높은 세금을 부과함으로써, 국민들은 추가 비용에 대한 부담을 갖게 될 것이고, 그래서 그들은 이러한 해로운 제품들의 구매를 중단할 것입니다.

ANSWERS AND SCRIPT

샘플 에세이 1
세금은 그들이 살고 있는 나라를 지원하기 위해 시민들에 의해 지불된다. 이 세금들로부터, 정부는 국민들의 복지를 향상시키기 위해 그 돈을 사용한다. 담배와 술에 대한 세금 인상이 시민들의 건강을 유지하는 데 도움이 된다면, 정부가 그러한 세금을 부과하는 것은 허용된다. 리차드가 말했듯이, 정부는 엄마와 같아서 시민들이 건강한 삶을 살 수 있도록 그들을 감시해야 한다. 게다가, 만약 국민들이 담배와 술 때문에 건강이 좋지 않다는 것을 알게 된다면, 정부는 결국 더 많은 돈을 쓰게 될 것이다. 국가는 더 많은 환자를 수용하기 위해 병원과 같은 더 많은 의료 시설을 건설해야 할 것이고, 그러한 시설의 건설과 유지는 시민들로부터 더 많은 세금을 요구할 것이다. 그러므로, 질병과 질병을 예방하는 동시에 추가적인 기반 시설을 만들기 위해 추가적인 세금을 지불하지 않기 위해, 정부는 건강에 좋지 않은 제품에 대한 세금을 인상해야 한다.
155단어

샘플 에세이 2
"국민을 위해, 국민에 의해"라는 유명한 속담이 있습니다 이것은 단순히 사람들이 그들에게 무엇이 좋은지 결정해야 한다고 말한다. 정부는 시민들의 생활 방식을 방해하려고 할 수도 있지만, 그들은 그들에게 무엇을 하라고 말할 권리가 없다. 따라서, 건강에 좋지 않은 제품에 대한 증가된 세금은 사람들의 자유와 권리를 침해하는 것이다. 나는 사람들이 그들의 몸에 무엇을 할 수 있는지 결정해야 한다는 마리아의 말에 동의한다. 덧붙이고 싶은 것은 그들의 결정에서 오는 결과가 무엇이든 그들의 책임이 되어야 한다는 것이다. 만약 개인들이 술을 마시고 담배를 피워서 그들의 몸을 해치기로 결정한다면, 그렇게 하게 내버려 두도록 한다. 그들은 내일이 없는 것처럼 살고 인생을 즐기고 있다. 하지만, 이러한 개인들이 건강 관리나 재활 프로그램의 부족을 정부의 탓으로 돌리지 말아야 한다는 것도 주목해야 한다. 결국, 그것은 그들의 자유였고 그들은 그러한 건강에 해로운 제품들을 소비하기로 결정했다. 그래서 사람들은 그들의 몸에 원하는 것은 무엇이든 할 수 있는 자유가 주어져야 하고, 정부가 그들의 행동을 통제하기 위해 더 높은 세금을 시행하는 것은 잘못된 것입니다.
188단어

Page.112~116

연습 5
교수는 기술 수업을 하는 중이다.
교수의 질문에 답하는 글을 쓰시오.

당신의 답변에서 다음을 수행해야 한다:
- 당신의 의견을 표현하고 지지한다
- 토론에 기여한다

유효한 응답에는 최소 100개의 단어가 포함된다.
당신에게는 그것을 쓸 시간이 10분 주어질 것이다.

브라운 박사
기술은 지난 수십 년 동안 매우 많이 발전했습니다. 인터넷의 창조는 사람들에게 풍부한 정보를 제공했습니다. 전기로 달리는 효율적인 자동차의 건설은 대기 오염을 해결하는 데 한 걸음을 내디뎠습니다. 최근의 열풍은 메타버스와 그것이 전 세계 사람들과의 인간의 상호작용을 어떻게 변화시킬 것인가에 관한 것입니다. 수많은 기술적 성과 중에서 어떤 것이 가장 큰 영향을 미쳤다고 생각합니까? 그 이유는 무엇입니까?

마티
저는 공기부양정이 가장 큰 영향을 미쳤다고 생각합니다. 비록 그것이 아직 완벽하지는 않지만, 호버크래프트의 발명은 사람들이 차량을 바꿀 필요 없이 물과 육지를 횡단할 수 있게 해주었습니다. 또한, 공기부양정의 사용은 다음과 같은 것들을 검토하는데 효과적인 것으로 증명되었습니다. 38선이 북한과 남한을 가르는 남한에서만, 공기부양정이 들판에 심어진 위험한 지뢰를 제거하는 데 사용되었습니다.

제니퍼
소셜 미디어 플랫폼은 분명 가장 중요한 기술적 성과여야 합니다. Youtube, Facebook, Instagram과 같은 플랫폼은 전 세계의 모든 사람들을 연결했습니다. 정보가 교환될 뿐만 아니라, 여러분과 같은 관심사나 취미를 공유하는 사람들과 새로운 관계를 형성할 수 있습니다.

샘플 에세이 1
고대 인류 문명은 서로 다른 문화 간의 정보 교환으로 번창할 수 있다. 이 요소는 현대 세계에서 여전히 중요하다. 그래서 나는 인터넷의 발명이 가장 큰 기술적 성과라고 생각한다. 제니퍼는 소셜 미디어 플랫폼을 가장 위대한 발명품으로 언급하지만, 인터넷은 소셜 미디어 플랫폼의 기반이다. 인터넷이 없다면, 사용자들은 그들의 사진이나 상태를 온라인에 올릴 수 없을 것이다. 마티는 공기부양정이 가장 큰 영향을 미쳤다고 말했다. 하지만 사람들은 어디서 그런 독특한 자동차를 만들 수 있는 정보를 얻었을까? 물론, 그것은 인터넷에서 온 것이다. 인터넷이 다른 모든 기술 발전을 위한 토대를 제공했다는 것은 분명하므로, 월드 와이드 웹이 가장 큰 영향을 미쳤다는 것은 의심의 여지가 없다.
 132단어

샘플 에세이 2
그 교수는 몇 가지 중요한 기술적 성과를 열거한다. 그래도 가장 큰 영향을 준 기술은 백신이라고 생각한다. 19세기까지, 사람들은 백신이 무엇인지 알지 못했고 그들이 병에 걸렸을 때 두려워했다. 질병이 그들의 생명을 앗아가지 않기를 바라는 것이다. 하지만, 백신의 발명으로, 사람들에게는 그들을 공격하는 것이 무엇이든 극복할 수 있다는 희망이 주어졌다. 예를 들어, 코로나19 바이러스가 처음으로 희생자들의 생명을 앗아가기 시작했을 때, 피해자들은 임박한 죽음을 두려워했다. 하지만 1년 안에 백신이 만들어졌고 많은 생명을 구했다. 이 코로나19 백신은 전 세계 수백만 명의 생명을 구했다. 다른 어떤 기술 발전도 그렇게 많은 사람들에 의해 사용되지 않았다. 따라서 백신은 가장 큰 기술적 진보로 간주되어야 한다.
 136단어

Actual Test 01

Page.120

Reading

Question 1 of 2

인구가 증가하고 도시가 팽창함에 따라, 도로와 건물의 건설로 인해 동물들의 서식지는 파괴되고, 동물들은 서식지가 상실된다. 이러한 동물들을 구조하기 위한 방법으로는 동물들을 안전한 환경으로 옮기는 방법이 제시되었다. 그러나 이러한 방법이 실용적이지 않다는 수많은 증거들이 있다.

우선, 동물들을 새로운 장소로 이동시키는 것은 개체 수 과잉을 초래할 수 있다. 새로운 환경은 이미 잘 균형 잡힌 생태계와 먹이 도식이 갖춰져 수많은 종들이 살고 있는 장소이다. 구조된 동물들이 들어오게 되면, 개체 수 과잉 문제가 생기기 마련이고 동물들은 자원을 놓고 서로 경쟁하게 될 것이다. 이러한 경쟁은 식량, 물, 거주지가 부족하게 될 것이므로 동물의 감소를 유발할 것이다. 그러므로 이주 해결책은 결국 동물들이 개체 수 과잉 상태가 되게 만들고, 결과적으로 극심한 경쟁으로 인해 굶어 죽게 될 것이다.

또한, 동물들의 이주는 새로운 환경에 바람직하지 않은 질병들을 퍼트리게 될 것이다. 동물들은 수많은 다양한 질병들을 옮기므로, 새로운 환경으로 옮겨질 때, 그들도 모르게 질병 또한 옮기게 될 것이다. 새로운 환경에 있는 동물들은 그러한 질병에 노출된 적이 없고, 따라서 관련 면역이 거의 없기 때문에 이는 매우 중대한 문제이다. 예를 들어, 중국 본토에서 샌디에이고 동물원으로 옮겨진 멸종 위기의 동물이 변형된 조류 독감을 옮겼고, 동물원의 수많은 동물들이 질병에 걸리게 되었다고 보고된 사례가 있다.

마지막으로, 동물들을 사로잡는 과정에서 동물들이 상처 입거나 죽게 되는 경우가 발생할 수 있다. 다른 장소로 옮기기 위해서, 반드시 첫 번째로 동물들을 포획해야 한다. 신경 안정제 화살은 더 크고 사나운 동물들에게 사용되지만, 때로는 신경 안정제의 양이 지나칠 수 있어 그것을 맞은 동물이 심장마비를 일으킬 수 있다. 또한, 동물들을 잡기 위해 설치된 덫은 한번 잡힌 동물에게 적절한 물과 공간을 제공하지 못할 것이다. 동물이 덫에 걸렸을 때, 때로는 사람들이 그것들을 풀어 주는데 며칠이 걸리기도 하지만, 그들이 도착하는 동안, 동물들은 이미 탈수 상태이거나 밀폐된 공간에서 신체적인 손상을 입었을 것이다.

Actual Test 01

Page.121

Listening

Question 1 of 2

(Female Professor)
There is a debate over the best way to save endangered species. One method that has been proposed is the relocation of the animals. The problems mentioned in the reading are actually not that big of a deal. As long as proper procedures are carried out, transporting the animals to a new home will be the most viable method.

Concerning the issue of overpopulation, this can easily be solved by creating new habitats or increasing the capacity of the environments. Barren land can be converted into habitats for animals that do not require much plant and water, such as desert reptiles and camels. This barren land has never been occupied by other animals, so overpopulation will not be a concern as competition for whatever resources that remain will not occur. Also, the carrying capacity of the new location can be increased by artificial means. Artificial coral reefs have been used for decades to accommodate fish and other marine life that have been moved to a new location when their old home was destroyed from water pollution. This helps the new environment support the new animals that have moved in, at the same time allowing the original inhabitants to continue on with their life.

Furthermore, the spread of disease can be prevented with careful monitoring. Once the animals move to the new location, they can be situated in separate areas to prevent any pathogens from breaking out. Experts can frequently visit the areas and if they notice any irregularities in the animal's health, they can immediately remove the species from the environment. Also, vaccines and shots can be administered to the animals before they are moved to make sure that they will not carry any known diseases to their new home.

Lastly, injury and death can be prevented as well. When making the traps, trap makers can make water dispensers inside so that the animals do not become dehydrated. Nowadays, traps have been made with GPS trackers and notification systems so that as soon as an animal is caught, experts can rush to the scene and retrieve the animal. Also, instead of using chemical tranquilizers with a chance that the dosage can be off, natural and herbal tranquilizers can be used to induce the animal to sleep. Lemon balm, Hops, and California Poppy have been effective at putting animals to sleep without turning to chemical tranquilizers that might kill them with the wrong dosage.

멸종 위기의 종들을 구하기 위한 최선의 방법에 대해 여러 논의가 있다. 제안된 한 가지 방법은 동물들의 이주이다. 읽기 지문에 언급된 문제점들은 사실 그다지 큰 문제가 아니다. 적절한 절차들이 이뤄지는 한, 동물들을 새로운 서식지로 운송하는 것은 가장 생존 가능성을 높일 것이다.

개체 수 과잉에 대해 살펴보면, 이는 새로운 서식지를 만들거나 기존 환경의 수용성을 증가시키는 방법으로 쉽게 해결될 수 있다. 척박한 땅은 사막 파충류나 낙타 같이 식물과 물을 많이 필요로 하지 않는 동물들의 서식지로 바뀔 수 있다. 이러한 척박한 땅은 다른 동물들에 의해 채워진 적이 없기 때문에, 남아있는 자원에 대한 경쟁이 생겨나지 않을 것이므로, 개체 수 과잉은 걱정거리가 되지 않는다. 또한, 새로운 장소의 수용 가능성은 인공적인 방법에 의해 증가할 수 있다. 인공 산호 암초는 수질 오염에 의해 자신들의 오래된 서식지가 파괴되어 새로운 장소로 이주한 물고기와 해양 생물들을 수용하기 위해서 수 십 년간 사용되었다. 이것은 새로운 환경에 이주한 새로운 동물들을 지원함과 동시에, 원래의 거주자들이 그들의 삶을 계속할 수 있도록 도와준다.

더 보자면, 질병의 확산은 세심한 모니터링으로 막을 수 있다. 동물들이 새로운 장소로 이동할 때, 그들은 병원균이 나오는 것을 막기 위해 분리된 장소에 놓일 수 있다. 전문가들은 이 지역을 자주 방문할 수 있으며, 만약 그들이 동물의 건강에 어떤 문제가 있는 것을 발견하면, 그들은 즉시 환경에서 그 동물들을 제거할 수 있다. 또한, 백신과 주사는 동물들이 어떤 질병도 새로운 서식지로 옮기지 않도록 하기 위해 이동하기 전에 투여될 수 있다.

마지막으로 부상과 사망도 예방할 수 있다. 덫을 만들 때, 덫 제조사들은 동물들이 탈수되지 않도록 안에 급수기를 달아줄 수 있다. 요즘은 GPS 추적기와 알림 시스템으로 덫을 만들어 동물이 잡히자마자 전문가가 현장으로 달려와 회수할 수 있도록 하고 있다. 또 투여량이 잘못될 가능성이 있는 화학 안정제를 사용하는 대신 천연 및 한방 안정제를 사용해 동물이 잠을 잘 수 있도록 유도할 수 있다. 레몬밤, 홉스, 캘리포니아 파피 등은 잘못된 복용량으로 동물을 죽일 수 있는 화학적 신경 안정제에 의지하지 않고 동물을 재우는 데 효과적이었다.

Actual Test 01

Page.126

00:10:00

교수는 사회 과목을 가르치는 중이다.
교수의 질문에 답하는 글을 쓰시오.

당신의 답변에서 다음을 수행해야 한다:
- 당신의 의견을 표현하고 지지한다
- 토론에 기여한다

유효한 응답에는 최소 100개의 단어가 포함된다.
당신에게는 그것을 쓸 시간이 10분 주어질 것이다.

콕스 박사
Ponce de Leon이 젊음의 샘을 찾기 시작했을 때, 인류의 장수에 대한 탐구가 시작되었습니다. 불행하게도 영원한 젊음의 마법의 샘은 존재하지 않기 때문에, 약과 약은 사람들이 더 오래 살 수 있도록 기대 수명을 늘렸습니다. 보통 사람들에게, 좋은 식단과 지속적인 운동은 한 사람의 수명을 연장시키기에 충분합니다. 당신은 이 둘 중 어느 것이 더 중요하다고 생각합니까? 왜죠?

엘리엇
요즘, 메뉴들은 음식을 먹는 사람들이 주문한 칼로리가 얼마나 되는지를 보여줍니다. 이것은 사회가 좋은 식단을 얼마나 강조하는지 보여줍니다. 나이, 몸무게, 키에 따라 사람이 섭취할 수 있는 칼로리의 양에는 제한이 있습니다. 만약 그들이 필요한 것보다 더 많은 칼로리를 소비한다면, 그들은 비만이 될 것입니다. 또는, 만약 그들이 최소한의 과일과 야채, 그리고 너무 많은 고기와 같은 불균형한 식사를 한다면, 그들의 건강은 악화될 것입니다. 그래서 좋은 식단을 먹는 것은 사람의 수명을 연장시킬 것입니다.

존
저는 매일 조깅을 합니다. 가끔 가벼운 달리기를 한 후에 농구를 하곤 했습니다. 이것은 운동이 나에게 얼마나 중요한지를 보여줍니다. 지속적인 운동으로, 사람들은 그들이 얼마나 많이 먹든 간에, 건강을 유지할 것입니다. 결국, 그들은 달리기를 하러 나가서 칼로리를 소모할 수 있습니다. 저는 먹는 것을 좋아하기 때문에 건강한 삶을 살 수 있도록 매일 운동을 합니다.

Actual Test 01

통합 샘플 에세이
독서 지문은 동물들을 더 안전한 서식지로 옮겨 구조하는 것은 실용적인 해결책이 아니라고 주장한다. 하지만, 듣기 지문은 적절한 절차가 수행되는 한, 동물들을 재배치하는 것이 가장 실행 가능한 방법이라고 주장한다.

우선, 저자는 동물들을 새로운 서식지로 이동시키는 것이 인구 과잉을 초래할 것이라고 주장한다. 새로운 환경은 이미 다른 종들의 서식지이기 때문에, 유기체들은 자원을 위해 서로 경쟁할 것이고 인구 과잉이 발생할 것이다. 그 경쟁은 최소한의 자원이 있기 때문에 동물들의 멸종으로 이어질 것이다. 반면에, 화자는 새로운 서식지를 만들거나 환경의 용량을 늘리면 문제가 해결될 것이라고 말하면서 이 주장을 반박한다. 척박한 땅은 사막 파충류나 낙타처럼 식물과 물을 많이 필요로 하지 않는 유기체의 서식지로 바뀔 수 있다. 그래서 인구 과잉은 문제가 되지 않을 것이다. 또한 인공적인 방법을 통해 환경의 운반 용량을 늘릴 수 있다. 인공 산호초는 물고기와 다른 해양 생물들이 새로운 집에 적응하는 것을 도와주면서 오랫동안 사용되어 왔다.

게다가, 저자는 동물들을 재배치하는 것이 새로운 환경에 원치 않는 질병을 퍼뜨릴 것이라고 언급한다. 동물들은 질병의 매개체이기 때문에, 그들은 자신도 모르게 그들의 새로운 집으로 질병을 옮길 것이다. 새로운 서식지에 있는 동물들은 질병에 노출된 적이 없기 때문에 면역력이 없을 것이다. 반대로, 강사는 세심한 모니터링이 질병의 확산을 막을 수 있다고 말하면서 이에 반대한다. 동물들이 새로운 집으로 이사할 때, 그들은 질병이 퍼지는 것을 막기 위해 별도의 장소에 배치될 수 있다. 만약 전문가들이 동물들에게 잘못된 점을 발견한다면, 그들은 환경으로부터 그 종을 이동시킬 수 있다. 또한, 알려진 질병이 새로운 환경으로 옮겨지지 않도록 백신과 주사를 놓을 수 있다.

게다가, 본문은 그 유기체들이 포획되는 동안 부상을 입거나 죽을 가능성이 있다고 주장한다. 재배치하기 위해서는 먼저 동물들을 잡아야 하지만, 신경안정제의 잘못된 투여량이나 부적절한 덫은 동물들에게 더 많은 해를 끼칠 것이다. 반대로, 그 강의는 부상과 죽음도 예방할 수 있다고 말하면서 이 주장에 이의를 제기한다. 덫을 만드는 사람들은 우리 안에 물 분사기를 만들 수 있고, GPS 추적기는 동물들을 회수하기 위해 우리에 부착될 수 있다. 또한, 화학적 신경안정제를 사용하는 대신에, 사람들은 동물이 잠을 자도록 유도하기 위해 천연 및 허브 신경안정제를 사용할 수 있다. 레몬밤, 홉, 그리고 캘리포니아 양귀비는 효과적인 천연 신경안정제이다.
426단어

학술 토론 샘플 에세이
사람의 건강을 유지하기 위해 상호 작용하는 몇 가지 요인이 있다. 하지만, 가장 중요한 측면은 좋은 식단이다. 몸이 제 기능을 할 수 있도록 적절한 양의 칼로리와 함께 균형 잡힌 식사를 해야 한다. 엘리엇이 그녀의 반응에서 언급했듯이, 너무 많은 칼로리를 소비하는 것은 비만을 초래할 것이다. 게다가, 만약 몸이 비만이라면, 그들은 심지어 움직이고 일상적인 활동을 하는 데 어려움을 겪을 것이다. 이것은 적절한 영양 섭취가 운동을 성취할 수 있게 해준다는 사실을 지적한다. 그래서 사람들은 그들이 얼마나 많은 운동을 하는지 보다 그들이 먹는 것에 우선순위를 두어야 한다는 것이 이치에 맞다. 격렬한 운동은 장수를 위해 권장되는 반면, 개인들은 그들의 일상적인 집안일로부터 충분한 운동을 얻는다. 집을 청소하고, 학교에 걸어가거나, 계단을 오르는 것은 충분한 운동 이상이다. 그래서 사람들이 균형 잡힌 식사를 하는 것은 필수적이다.
144단어

Actual Test 02

Page.134

00:03:00

요즘, 환경 운동가들은 지구 온난화에 대해 매우 우려하고 있다. 전 세계적으로 기온이 상승함에 따라, 우리 사회의 많은 부문들이 기후 변화로 인한 피해를 목격했다. 비록 몇몇 회의론자들이 지구 온난화가 현실적이지 않다고 주장하지만, 환경론자들은 지구 온난화가 매우 현실적이고 여러 지역에서 볼 수 있다고 주장한다.

첫째, 높은 해수면은 기후가 기온이 상승했음을 나타낸다. 북극과 남극을 덮고 있는 빙하는 수십 년에 걸쳐 사진을 찍은 위성 사진으로 증명될 수 있기 때문에 크기가 감소했다. 예를 들어, 남극대륙은 3조 톤 이상의 손실을 보았다. 지난 25년 동안의 얼음. 빙하에서 녹아내린 물과 빙하에서 떨어져 나온 빙산은 온도가 확실히 증가했다는 것을 보여준다.

둘째, 지구 온난화는 지난 몇 년 동안 심각한 기상 현상을 유발했다. 미국 내에서는 기상 차이로 인해 중부 평원을 휩쓸고 있는 거대한 토네이도가 더 빈번하게 발생했다. 동남아시아 국가들에서, 허리케인과 태풍은 홍수와 폭우를 일으켰고, 그것은 휩쓸렸다. 마을들과 세계의 다른 지역에서는, 눈보라가 엄청난 양의 눈과 얼음 때문에 밖에 나갈 수 없는 시민들을 그들의 집에 가두었다. 이 모든 날씨 사건들은 지구 온난화로 인한 심각한 날씨 차이에서만 발생할 수 있다.

셋째, 지구 기온의 상승은 식량 부족을 초래했다. 기온이 상승하면서 세계의 특정 지역에서는 가뭄이 증가하고 비가 적게 오는 것을 목격했는데, 이것은 농부들에게 불행한 일이다. 이런 불모지 같은 상황에서 식량 생산량은 사상 최저치에 이르렀다. 아프리카의 국가들은 특히 지구 온난화로 고통받고 있고 많은 국제 구호 단체들은 영양실조 국가들에게 지속적으로 음식과 물을 제공하고 있다.

ANSWERS AND SCRIPT

Actual Test 02

Page.135

Listening

Question 1 of 2

(Male Professor)
Global warming is a myth that has been exaggerated by environmentalists, celebrities, and politicians. What we are experiencing now is a natural cycle that has been occurring on our planet for millions of years. The areas mentioned in the reading are therefore misled and can be proven erroneous.

It is true that we have witnessed an increased sea level within the past few years. But this is because we are in a period called the post-ice age. Earth's history has shown us that our planet undergoes an ice age, then a melting period, and then returning to another ice age and the cycle continues, switching from ice to no ice. The melting of the glaciers and icebergs only prove that Earth is in that no ice period, and soon another ice age will envelope the globe. That doesn't mean that mankind will perish and the Earth will turn to a solid ball of ice, no. Perhaps the location of cities will move more closer to the equator, since it is closest to the sun. So global warming is not the cause, rather it's a natural cycle that is causing the water levels to rise.

Also, the severe weather events are caused by a different factor. Manmade structures have created temperature gradients between the ground and the air. With more cement buildings and asphalt paved roads, the temperature of the ground increases abnormally. For instance, asphalt is black, which is a color that absorbs the most energy compared to other colors. On a hot summer day, the temperature of an asphalt can be as hot as 62 degrees Celsius. When the ground is this hot and the air is cold, the temperature difference creates massive tornadoes and other unnatural weather phenomenon. If humans develop less energy absorbent material to construct the buildings and roads, then there would be a definite decrease in severe weather events. So global warming has nothing to do with this as well.

Finally, food shortage is yet another result of man. The human population does not increase in a linear fashion. It increases exponentially. So with the human population on Earth at 7.8 billion, no wonder there is a lack of resource. The traditional methods of growing food is outpaced by the growing numbers, so these days, scientists have come up with nontraditional methods to grow food. For example, beverages that contain the nutrition of one meal have been invented to be consumed, rather than chowing down on solid food. This has actually become popular amongst individuals who wish to go on a diet and maintain a healthier body weight. Thus global warming did not contribute to food shortage.

지구 온난화는 환경 운동가, 유명인, 정치인 등에 의해 과장된 신화이다. 우리가 지금 경험하고 있는 것은 수백만 년 동안 지구에서 일어나고 있는 자연적 주기이다. 따라서 이 글에서 언급된 부분들은 오해이며, 오류로 판명될 것이다.

우리가 지난 몇 년 사이에 해수면 상승을 목격한 것은 사실이다. 그러나 이것은 우리가 후빙기라고 불리는 시대에 있기 때문이다. 지구의 역사는 지구가 빙하 시대를 거쳐 해빙기로, 그 후 또 다른 빙하 시대로 돌아가는 순환이 계속되어 빙하기와 해빙기가 계속 바뀐다는 것을 보여 주었다. 해빙과 빙산은 지구가 해빙기에 있다는 것을 증명하는 것일 뿐이며, 조만간 또 다른 빙하기가 지구를 뒤덮을 것이다. 그렇다고 해서 인류가 멸망한다거나 지구가 단단한 얼음덩어리로 변한다는 뜻은 아니다. 아마도 도시들의 위치는 적도에 더 가까워질 것인데 그 이유는 태양에 가장 근접할 것이기 때문이다. 따라서 수위 상승을 초래하는 원인은 지구 온난화가 아니라 자연적인 주기이다.

또한 심각한 기상 사건들은 다른 요인들에 의해 발생한다. 인공 구조물은 땅과 공기 사이에 온도 차이를 만들어낸다. 시멘트 건물과 아스팔트 포장도로가 많아지면 지반 온도가 비정상적으로 상승한다. 예를 들어 아스팔트는 검정색인데 이는 다른 색에 비해 에너지를 가장 많이 흡수하는 색이다. 더운 여름날, 아스팔트의 온도는 섭씨 62도 정도까지 뜨거울 수 있다. 지면은 이렇게 뜨겁고 공기는 차가울 때의 온도 차이는 거대한 토네이도와 다른 비정상적인 기상 현상을 일으킨다. 만약 인간이 건물과 도로를 건설하는데 에너지를 덜 흡수하는 물질을 개발한다면, 심각한 기상 현상들이 확실히 줄어들 것이다. 따라서 지구 온난화는 이것과도 아무 상관이 없다.

마지막으로, 식량 부족은 인간이 만들어낸 또 다른 결과물이다. 인류는 정비례로 증가하지 않고, 기하급수적으로 늘어난다. 그래서 지구상의 인구가 78억이기 때문에 자원이 부족한 것은 당연하다. 식량을 재배하는 전통적인 방법들은 증가하는 인구를 따라잡을 수 없기 때문에, 요즈음 과학자들은 식량을 재배하는 과거와 다른 방법을 고안해냈다. 예를 들어, 한 끼의 영양분을 함유한 음료는 고형식으로 먹는 것 대신 마실 수 있게 발명되었다. 이것은 실제로 다이어트를 하고 더 건강한 체중을 유지하기를 원하는 사람들 사이에서 인기를 끌었다. 따라서 지구 온난화는 식량 부족에 기여하지 않았다.

Actual Test 02

Page.140

00:10:00

교수는 교육에 대한 수업을 하는 중이다.
교수의 질문에 답하는 글을 쓰시오.

당신의 답변에서 다음을 수행해야 한다:
- 당신의 의견을 표현하고 지지한다
- 토론에 기여한다

유효한 응답에는 최소 100개의 단어가 포함된다.
당신에게는 그것을 쓸 시간이 10분 주어질 것이다.

벨딩 교수
매년, 대학들은 그들의 교육을 향상시키기 위해 정부와 부유한 졸업생들에 의해 자금과 후원을 받습니다. 여전히, 학교들은 그들의 교육 개혁을 보완할 재정적인 자원이 부족합니다. 자금이 필요한 많은 분야가 있습니다. 교실과 같은 학술 시설, 빔 프로젝터와 같은 장비, 스포츠 및 운동 프로그램 등입니다. 대학들은 자원의 우선순위를 어디에 두어야 합니까? 그리고 그 이유는 무엇인가요?

잭
학교는 스포츠와 운동 프로그램에 자원을 집중해야 합니다. 요즘, 대학들은 그들의 스포츠 팀으로 인기가 있습니다. 대학 미식축구와 농구는 전국 텔레비전 프로그램에서 보여지고 미국 전역의 사람들은 그들이 가장 좋아하는 대학 팀들이 경기하는 것을 보기 위해 채널을 맞추고 있습니다. 만약 대학들이 스포츠와 운동 프로그램에 그들의 자금을 우선시한다면, 더 많은 학생들이 학교에 다니기를 원할 것이고, 이것은 재정적인 이익 뿐만 아니라 학교 이미지를 높일 것입니다.

켈리
저는 교실이 중요하다는 것에 동의하지만, 적절한 장비 없이는 완성되지 않을 것입니다. 교실은 그저 방일 뿐입니다. 하지만, 일단 그것이 프로젝터, 컴퓨터, 그리고 스피커와 같은 첨단 기술 장비들로 제공되면, 교수들과 학생들 모두가 수업을 가르치고 배우는 데 더 쉬운 시간을 가질 것입니다. 결국, 학교는 제대로 배우는 곳이어야 합니다.

Actual Test 02

통합 샘플 에세이

이 독서 지문은 지구 온난화가 매우 현실적이며 여러 지역에서 관찰될 수 있다고 주장한다. 그러나 듣기 지문은 읽기에서 언급된 요점들이 잘못되었다고 주장한다.

우선, 저자는 높은 해수면은 기후가 기온이 상승했음을 의미한다고 주장한다. 빙하의 크기가 감소했다. 수십 년 동안의 위성 사진이 그 증거이다. 빙하에서 녹은 물과 빙하에서 분리된 빙산은 온도가 상승하고 있다는 결론을 내린다. 반면에, 화자는 인간이 빙하기 이후라고 불리는 시기에 있다고 말하면서 이 주장을 반박한다. 지구의 역사는 빙하기와 녹는 시기의 반복을 보여주며, 인간은 빙하기가 없는 시기에 있다. 또 다른 빙하기가 온다고 해도, 지구는 얼음덩어리로 변하지 않을 것이다. 도시의 위치는 태양에 더 가깝기 때문에 적도에 더 가까워질 것이다. 따라서 수위가 상승하는 것은 지구 온난화가 아니라 지구가 겪고 있는 자연적인 순환일 뿐이다.

게다가, 저자는 심각한 기상 현상이 표면화되었다고 언급한다. 미국에서는 토네이도가 더 자주 발생하고 거대해지고 있다. 허리케인, 태풍, 그리고 눈보라는 지구 온난화로 인한 중요한 날씨 차이로 인해 더 자주 나타났다. 반대로, 강사는 악천후는 실제로 인간에 의해 발생한다고 말하면서 이것에 반대한다. 건물들은 공기와 땅 사이에 엄청난 온도 구배를 만들었다. 더운 여름날, 아스팔트는 섭씨 62도까지 뜨거울 수 있는데, 이것은 토네이도와 다른 부자연스러운 날씨 사건들을 만들 수 있다. 인간이 건물과 도로를 위해 에너지 흡수성이 낮은 물질을 만드는 한, 부자연스러운 기상 현상은 더 이상 존재하지 않을 것이다.

게다가, 이 글은 지구 온난화가 식량 부족을 초래했다고 주장한다. 더 높은 기온과 가뭄, 그리고 최소한의 비가 농부들에게 문제를 가져왔다. 식량 생산량이 사상 최저치에 도달했다. 반대로, 그 강의는 식량 부족은 인류가 만든 문제라고 말하면서 이 주장에 도전한다. 인간의 인구는 기하급수적으로 증가하기 때문에 전통적인 식량 재배 방법은 증가하는 수치에 의해 앞지릅니다. 오늘날, 증가하는 숫자에 맞추기 위해 한 끼 식사의 영양을 포함하는 음료와 같은 비전통적인 방법들이 생산되고 있다. 사실, 이것은 다이어트에 종사하거나 더 건강한 삶을 살기 위해 노력하는 사람들 사이에서 인기를 얻었다. 그래서 지구 온난화는 식량 부족과 아무런 관련이 없다.

414단어

학술 토론 샘플 에세이

리소스가 제한적인 경우 가장 효과적인 결과를 내기 위해 어디에 우선순위를 두어야 하는지 아는 것이 중요하다. 대학이 자원의 우선순위를 정해야 한다면, 학교는 교수들을 고용하고 유지하는 데 초점을 맞추는 것이 가장 좋다. 나는 대학이 스포츠 팀으로 인기가 있다는 젝의 말에 동의한다. 하지만, 대학은 그들의 학문적인 프로그램과 업적으로 알려져야 한다. 이것은 명문 출신의 저명한 교수들에 의해 성취될 수 있다. 예를 들어, 하버드나 예일 같은 아이비리그 학교들은 전 세계 학생들에 의해 추구된다. 그들은 학교의 학업적 우수성 때문에 학교에 다니기를 원하며, 축구나 농구를 하기를 원하지 않는다. 이 학교들의 수업은 노벨상 후보자들과 놀라운 업적을 가진 교수들에 의해 진행된다. 대학들은 교수들이 근무 조건과 급여에 만족하는지 확인하고, 대학에 기여할 교수진을 추가로 채용하는 방안을 모색해야 한다. 그러므로, 학교는 그들의 자원을 그들의 교직원들에게 집중하는 것이 필수적이다.

168단어

Actual Test 03

Page.148

Reading

Question 1 of 2

요즘 학교에서는 학생들에게 교복을 입도록 하고 있다. 한국과 일본 같은 나라에서는, 중학생과 고등학생들이 그들이 다니는 학교를 대표하는 패션과 색상으로 옷을 입는다. 사실 교복을 입는 것에는 많은 이점이 있다.

첫째, 교복을 입는 것은 학생들의 안전을 보장한다. 범죄가 많은 나라에서 교복은 학생들이 패싸움이나 무기 은닉에 대해 걱정할 필요 없이 학교에 올 수 있도록 한다. 조직원들은 빨강, 파랑, 녹색과 같은 특정한 색상과 연관되어 있으며, 그러한 대담한 색을 입는 것은 착용자가 어떤 조직에 속하는지 나타낸다. 교복은 이러한 색깔을 숨기고 학교에서 폭력배들이 서로 경쟁하지 않도록 한다. 또한, 전통적인 일상복은 헐렁한 옷 아래에 무기를 숨기는 것을 도왔다. 그러나 교복은 헐렁하지 않기 때문에 더 이상 무기를 숨겨서 학교에 가져갈 수 없다. 그래서 교복을 입음으로써 학교에서의 안전이 보장된다.

둘째, 교복을 입음으로써 사회 경제적 불균형이 줄어든다. 최근 10대들 사이에서 유명 브랜드 옷이 인기를 끌고 있다. 이런 브랜드 제품들은 수백 달러다. 단순한 청바지는 300달러가 들 수도 있고 가슴에 작은 마크가 있는 단색 스웨터는 400달러가 들 수도 있다. 유명한 로고가 새겨진 이 옷을 입음으로써, 학생들은 그들의 사회 경제적 지위를 드러내고, 학교에서 격차가 생길 것이다. 그러한 옷을 살 여유가 있는 학생들은 그들 자신의 그룹을 형성하고 때로는 그러한 옷을 살 여유가 없는 다른 학생들을 깔보고 기피할 것이다. 교복은 모든 사람이 평등하게 보여지고 그러한 사회 경제적 불균형이 존재하지 않도록 한다.

셋째, 교복은 학업을 장려한다. 학생들이 매일 같은 옷을 입고 학교에 갈 때, 무엇을 입을지 고민하는데 드는 시간을 절약하여 퀴즈를 위한 공부 시간에 쓸 수 있다. 또한, 학생들은 옷을 사러 쇼핑하는 시간을 줄일 것이고, 그래서 공부를 위해 더 많은 시간을 절약할 수 있을 것이다. 학교에서, 학생들은 교복은 모든 사람에게 똑같이 보이기 때문에 자기가 어떻게 보이는지에 대해 걱정하지 않을 것이고, 그래서 그들은 정말로 중요한 것, 즉 공부에 집중할 수 있다.

Actual Test 03

Page.149

Listening

Question 1 of 2

(Male Professor)
School uniforms definitely provide benefits. However the points mentioned in the reading are erroneous as loopholes can be found within each of the benefits.

In regards to safety, school uniforms do not conceal gang membership. Even at school, gang members will huddle and gather in their own groups so different gangs can identify each other just by observation. Furthermore, although colors can be hidden by the uniforms, gang members imprint tattoos on their bodies, which can easily be identified when they wear short sleeved uniforms. Also, uniforms will not do much in preventing students from bringing weapons to school. If students manage to bring weapons, they would have done so by putting the items in their backpacks, or placing the weapons in concealed locations around school the previous night when no one is there to check. Therefore, wearing uniforms do little to prevent crime at school.

Moreover, socioeconomic status can still exist even when students wear uniforms. These days, shoes, backpacks, and accessories cost much more than regular clothes. Designer brand shoes can be well worth over $500 dollars, backpacks from luxurious brands can be around $1000 dollars, and watches can go from $1000 and up. These items can reveal the economic status of the students so there will still be socioeconomic disparities. The best method here would be to eliminate all personal articles of clothing and that the school not only provides uniforms, but the shoes and backpacks as well so that not a single item will show their economic status.

Finally, students will not concentrate on their studies when they are wearing school uniforms. Some people may think that because everyone will wear the same clothes there is no need to stand out. However this is actually misleading. When students are wearing the same clothes, they will find alternative means to stand out. Girls will put on flashier makeup while boys try to look tough by not buttoning their shirt or styling their hair differently. This will require constant attention, so students will be staring at mirrors and not focusing on their studies. Also, since students are limited from what they wear at school, they will in fact spend more time going out to shop for clothes because they will feel the need to make sure their casual clothes are the most fashionable amongst their friends when they meet outside of school. This will result in more time not being spent on studying.

ANSWERS AND SCRIPT

교복은 확실히 이점을 제공한다. 그러나 각 이점 안에서 허점을 발견할 수 있기 때문에 본문에서 언급된 요점들은 잘못되었다.

안전과 관련하여 교복은 갱단의 조직원임을 숨기지 않는다. 학교에서도 조직원들이 자신들의 특징대로 옹기종기 모여서 다른 조직원들이 관찰만 해도 서로를 알아볼 수 있다. 게다가 유니폼에 의해 색이 가려질 수 있지만, 폭력배들은 짧은 소매의 교복을 입었을 때 쉽게 알아볼 수 있는 문신을 자신의 몸에 새긴다. 또한, 교복은 학생들이 학교에 무기를 가지고 오는 것을 막는 데 별로 도움이 되지 않을 것이다. 학생들이 무기를 들고 오게 된다면, 그들은 그 무기들을 배낭에 넣거나, 점검하는 사람이 없는 전날 밤 학교 주변의 숨겨진 장소에 두는 방법을 이용했을 것이다. 그러므로 교복을 입는 것은 학교에서 범죄를 예방하는 데 거의 도움이 되지 않는다.

더구나 교복을 입어도 사회 경제적 지위는 여전히 존재할 수 있다. 요즘 신발, 배낭, 액세서리는 일반 옷보다 훨씬 비싸다. 디자이너 브랜드 신발의 가격은 500달러가 넘고, 명품 브랜드의 배낭은 1000달러 내외, 시계는 1000달러 이상이다. 이러한 항목들은 학생들의 경제적 상태를 드러낼 수 있기 때문에 사회 경제적 불균형이 여전히 존재할 것이다. 여기서 가장 좋은 방법은 모든 개인 의류를 없애고 학교가 교복뿐만 아니라 신발과 배낭도 제공해 단 한 가지 품목도 경제적 지위를 보여 주지 않는 것이다.

마지막으로, 학생들은 교복을 입을 때 공부에 집중하지 않을 것이다. 어떤 사람들은 모든 사람들이 같은 옷을 입어 눈에 띌 필요가 없다고 생각하지만, 이것은 사실 오해다. 학생들이 같은 옷을 입고 있을 때, 그들은 눈에 띌 수 있는 다른 방법을 찾을 것이다. 남학생들이 셔츠 단추를 채우지 않거나 머리를 다르게 스타일링하여 터프해 보이려고 노력하는 동안 여학생들은 더 번쩍이는 화장을 할 것이다. 이것은 계속 신경을 써야 하기 때문에 학생들은 거울을 들여다보고 공부에 집중하지 않을 것이다. 또한, 학생들은 학교에서 입는 옷에 제한이 있기 때문에, 실제로 옷을 사러 나가는 데 더 많은 시간을 보낼 것이다. 왜냐하면 그들이 학교 밖에서 만날 때 자신의 일상복이 친구들 사이에서 가장 유행하는 것이어야 한다고 느낄 것이기 때문이다. 이것은 공부에 더 많은 시간을 쓰지 않는 결과를 가져올 것이다.

Actual Test 03

Page.154

00:10:00

교수는 경영학 수업을 하는 중이다.
교수의 질문에 답하는 글을 쓰시오.

당신의 답변에서 다음을 수행해야 한다:
- 당신의 의견을 표현하고 지지한다
- 토론에 기여한다

유효한 응답에는 최소 100개의 단어가 포함된다.
당신에게는 그것을 쓸 시간이 10분 주어질 것이다.

스콧 박사
유행병과 장거리 통근이 시작되면서 원격 근무는 전 세계의 다양한 기업과 기업에서 표준 근무 환경이 되었습니다. 물론, 이것은 사람들이 서로 일하는 방식과 상호작용하는 방식을 바꾸기 때문에 일부 사람들에게는 여전히 새로운 것입니다. 그러므로, 회사들은 그들의 노동자들이 그들의 집에서 일하는 것을 허용하는 결정을 내리기 전에 모든 면을 고려해야 합니다. 당신 생각은 어때요? 원격 작업이 유용합니까? 아니면 더 많은 작업을 창출합니까?

짐
원격 작업이 확실히 유리합니다. 저는 사무실에서 하루의 일을 몇 시간 만에 끝낼 때가 있습니다. 하지만 저는 의무적으로 직장에 있어야 하기 때문에 지루하고 놀면서 시간을 낭비합니다. 하지만, 집에서 일하는 것은 제가 집안일을 돕거나 심지어 부업을 함으로써 생산적으로 여분의 시간을 보낼 수 있게 해줄 것입니다.

파멜라
저에게 원격 작업은 여전히 새로운 것입니다. 그리고 저는 새로운 것을 시도하는 것이 두렵습니다. 그래서 사무실에서 일하는 것이 저에게 훨씬 좋습니다. 당신은 일을 할 뿐만 아니라, 동료들과 개인적인 관계를 가질 수 있습니다. 한 사람이 같은 직장에서 몇 년을 일할 수 있기 때문에, 저는 직장에서 관계를 맺는 것이 중요하다고 생각합니다.

Actual Test 03

통합 샘플 에세이

독서 지문은 교복을 입는 것에 많은 이점이 있다고 주장한다. 하지만 듣기 지문은 읽기에서 언급된 요점에서 허점이 발견될 수 있다고 주장한다.

우선, 글쓴이는 교복이 안전을 보장한다고 주장한다. 교복은 학생들이 갱단 싸움이나 숨겨진 무기에 대해 걱정하지 않고 학교에 올 수 있게 해준다. 교복은 갱과 관련된 색깔을 숨길 것이고 그래서 학교에서 갱 구성원들 사이에 경쟁이 없을 것이다. 또한, 교복은 느슨하지 않기 때문에 무기가 숨겨져 학교에 반입되는 것을 막을 것이다. 반면, 발언자는 교복이 실제로 폭력조직원을 숨기지 않는다고 말하면서 이 주장을 반박한다. 갱단들은 그들 자신의 그룹에 함께 머물 것이고, 이것은 그들을 식별하는 데 도움이 될 것이다. 또한, 학생들이 짧은 소매의 교복을 입을 때 갱 문신을 볼 수 있을 것이다. 학생들은 또한 아무도 없는 전날 밤 학교 주변의 숨겨진 장소에 무기를 놓을 수 있기 때문에 학교에 무기를 가져오는 데 어려움이 없을 것이다. 그래서 교복을 입는 것은 학교에서 범죄를 예방하지 못한다.

게다가, 저자는 사회 경제적 차이를 줄일 수 있다고 언급한다. 명품 의류는 수백 달러가 될 수 있다. 이렇게 비싼 옷을 입음으로써, 학생들은 그들의 사회 경제적 지위를 드러내고 학교에서 격차가 생길 것이다. 교복은 모든 사람이 평등하다는 것을 확실히 할 것이다. 반대로, 강사는 교복을 입어도 사회경제적 차이가 여전히 보일 것이라고 말하면서 이것에 반대한다. 신발, 배낭, 그리고 액세서리들은 사실 천 달러 이상이 드는 옷보다 더 비싸다. 사회 경제적 격차를 숨기는 가장 좋은 방법은 학교에서 교복과 함께 신발과 배낭을 제공하여 단 한 벌의 옷도 그들의 경제적 지위를 보여주지 않도록 하는 것이다.

게다가, 본문은 교복이 더 많은 학업에 도움이 된다고 주장한다. 학생들은 그 날 무엇을 입을지 결정하지 않아도 됨으로써 매일 아침 시간을 절약할 수 있고 그들은 옷을 사는 데 더 적은 시간을 쓸 것이다. 절약된 이 시간은 그들의 공부에 투자될 수 있다. 심지어 학교에서도, 학생들은 그들이 어떻게 생겼는지에 대해 걱정할 필요가 없을 것이다, 왜냐하면 그들은 모두 똑같이 보일 것이기 때문에, 그들은 그들의 공부에 더 집중할 것이다. 반대로, 그 강의는 학생들이 같은 옷을 입을 때, 그들은 돋보일 다른 방법을 찾을 것이라고 말하면서 이 주장에 이의를 제기한다. 소녀들은 더 많은 화장을 하고 소년들은 그들의 머리 스타일을 다르게 할 것이다. 이것은 지속적인 관심을 필요로 할 것이고, 그래서 학생들은 학교 공부에 집중하지 않고 거울을 보는데 많은 시간을 보낼 것이다. 또한, 학생들은 학교 밖에서 친구들을 만날 때 더 멋을 부리기 위해 노력하기 때문에 쇼핑하는 데 더 많은 시간을 보낼 것이다. 그래서 학생들은 그들의 공부에 더 적은 시간을 쓸 것이다.
447단어

학술 토론 샘플 에세이

사람들은 근무 시간이 끝나면 출근 시간을 기록하고 퇴근 시간을 기록하는 데 익숙하다. 하지만 요즘에는, 그들은 원격 근무 덕분에 집에서 편안하게 되었다. 이러한 형태의 업무가 제공할 수 있는 많은 이점이 있다. 첫째, 소중한 시간을 절약할 수 있다. 짐은 그가 사무실에서 하루에 몇 시간만 일한다고 말했다. 중요한 것은 직원들이 출퇴근 시간에 출근해야 한다는 것이다. 차로 30분만 달려도 차로 출근할 수 있었던 것이 교통체증이 심하면 1시간이 될 수도 있다. 둘째, 근로자들은 자신을 위해 또는 가족과 함께 더 많은 시간을 보낼 수 있다. 사람들이 일과 삶의 균형을 강조함에 따라, 직원들은 집에서 일함으로써 이 균형을 얻을 수 있다. 그들은 일하는 동안 짧은 휴식을 취할 수 있고 취미생활이나 사랑하는 사람들과 이야기를 하며 시간을 보낼 수 있다. 그러므로, 집에서 원격으로 일하는 것에는 더 많은 이점이 있다.
155단어

Actual Test 04

Page.162

Reading

Question 1 of 2

개인 수송은 기술의 발달로 큰 발전을 이루었다. 스마트 카는 첨단 기계 공학과 어떤 형태의 인공 지능이 탑재된 컴퓨터를 활용한다. 비록 스마트 카가 완전한 잠재력을 보여 주지는 못하였지만, 가까운 미래에 전도유망한 이점들을 보여줄 것이라 확신한다.

스마트 카가 제공하는 한가지 이점은 교통의 흐름을 더 빠르게 하는 것이다. 스마트 카는 스스로 주행하기 때문에, 경로에 있는 차량들의 수나 속도에 근거하여, 목적지에 도착하기 위한 최선의 경로를 선택할 것이다. 결과적으로, 이동 시간은 더 짧아지고, 교통 흐름은 지속적으로 원활할 것이다. 또한, 인간 운전자들은 운전 중에 실수 할 가능성이 있다. 때때로, 그들은 졸아서 사고를 일으키거나 교통 흐름을 저해 할 수 있다. 아마추어 운전자들은 제한 속도 이하로 운전하는 경향이 있어, 교통 흐름도 느려 질 것이다.

또한, 스마트 카는 최소한의 유지비가 들 것이다. 스마트 카는 작은 문제가 드러나자마자 운전자들에게 경고를 보낸다. 차량 소유자들은 작은 문제가 심각하고 값 비싼 문제로 커지기 전에 적은 비용으로 정비소에 가서 문제를 해결할 수 있을 것이다. 게다가, 스마트 카는 인간 운전자보다 차량을 더 잘 다루기 때문에, 타이어, 엔진, 또는 브레이크 패달이 더 빨리 마모될 가능성이 낮을 것이고, 따라서 수리에 드는 비용을 최소화 하면서 더 오랜 기간 동안 차를 사용할 수 있을 것이다.

마지막으로, 스마트 카는 가솔린 연료에 의존하지 않고, 리튬 이온 전지로 주행한다. 지구는 가솔린으로 사용되는 화석 연료 자원이 한정적이기 때문에, 인간이 사용하는 화석 연료의 양을 줄이기 시작해야만 한다. 또한, 배터리로 주행하는 스마트 카는 어떠한 오염 물질도 생산하지 않는다. 가솔린으로 주행하는 자동차들이 탄소를 배출하여 환경 오염을 일으키는 반면, 배터리로 작동되는 자동차들은 환경에 해로울 수 있는 그 어떤 물질도 배출하지 않는다.

ANSWERS AND SCRIPT

Actual Test 04

Page.163

Listening

Question 1 of 2

(Male Professor)
Smart cars are not all bells and whistles. There has been increasing reports of smart car accidents all across the driving roads. Therefore, despite what people expect, smart cars will not be so beneficial even in the future.

First, smart cars will not help ease traffic flow. Even if the smart car is driving itself and chooses the optimal route to drive, driving conditions are constantly changing. A rush hour traffic may suddenly appear at an intersection, when just 10 minutes ago, there was none. An accident with a pedestrian might cause an entire road to shut down. So even if the smart car is alerted of the driving conditions, it will still encounter unexpected events which will slow the traffic. Also, one cannot ignore a human instinct. While a smart car's AI makes calculated driving routes, human drivers will use their experience and instinct to use different roads and avoid sudden traffic accident that could have occurred if they had used the road the smart car used.

Second, smart cars will not be cheap. Even if the smart car alerts the driver of minor problems, fixing that minor problem will be expensive. Since smart cars are not dominating the car market, their parts and repair are more expensive compared to traditional gasoline cars. Sometimes, mechanics might have to import the car parts from different countries because the smart cars are not in high demand in that country. Also, replacing the battery on a smart car is almost as expensive as the car itself. For example, a famous Japanese car maker Toyota introduced its smart car called Prius several years ago. After using the car for years, Prius owners found out that the battery replacement would cost more than ten thousand dollars. This is much more expensive than traditional car batteries, which is less than a hundred dollars.

Lastly, smart cars may not produce pollution while driving, but the lithium ion batteries used in the cars create one of the most hazardous wastes when the battery dies. The lithium ion batteries used by smart cars are not your average AA or AAA battery. They are huge. A battery that has been used will be thrown in the dumpsters, and when battery leakage occurs, the soil and groundwater will be affected immediately. Acid will leak out of the battery and everything surrounding the battery will be affected. So for a smart car battery, which is several hundred times in size compared to AA batteries, the effect would be much more devastating.

스마트 카는 완벽한 것이 아니다. 도로 곳곳에서 스마트 카 사고가 발생했다는 신고가 늘고 있다. 그러므로, 사람들의 기대에도 불구하고, 스마트 카는 미래에도 그다지 이롭지 않을 것이다.

첫째, 스마트 카는 교통 흐름을 완화시키는데 도움이 되지 않을 것이다. 스마트 카가 스스로 주행하고 운전하는데 있어 최적의 경로를 선택한다 하여도, 주행 여건은 끊임없이 변화하고 있다. 10분 전까지만 해도 아무것도 없던 교차로에서, 극심한 교통 체증이 갑자기 나타날 수 있다. 보행자와의 사고가 모든 도로를 폐쇄시킬 수도 있다. 그래서 스마트 카가 주행 여건에 대해 경고를 받는다 하더라도, 여전히 교통을 느리게 하는 예상치 못한 사건들을 만나게 될 것이다. 또한, 인간의 본능을 무시할 수 없다. 스마트 카의 AI가 주행 경로를 계산하는 동안, 인간 운전자들은 그들의 경험과 직관을 사용하여 다른 경로를 이용할 것이고, 스마트 카가 이용했던 도로를 사용함으로써 발생할 수 있는 갑작스러운 교통 사고를 피할 수 있다.

둘째, 스마트 카는 싸지 않을 것이다. 스마트 카가 운전자에게 작은 문제를 알려준다 하더라도, 이를 수리하는 비용은 비쌀 것이다. 스마트 카가 자동차 시장을 장악하고 있지 않기 때문에, 이러한 차량들의 부품과 수리는 기존 가솔린 차량들에 비해 비싸다. 스마트 카들의 수요가 높지 않기 때문에, 때때로 정비사들은 다른 나라에서 해당 차량의 부속품들을 수입해야 할 수도 있다. 또한 스마트 카의 배터리를 교체하는 것은 자동차 자체만큼이나 비싸다. 예를 들어, 일본의 유명한 자동차 제조업체인 도요타는 몇 년 전 프리우스라고 불리는 스마트 카를 출시했다. 몇 년 동안 이 차를 사용한 후, 프리우스 차주들은 배터리 교체비용이 만 달러 이상 든다는 것을 알게 되었다. 이는 100달러도 되지 않는 기존 자동차 배터리보다 훨씬 비싸다.

마지막으로, 스마트 카는 주행 중 오염 물질을 발생시키지 않을 수 있지만, 자동차에 사용되는 리튬 이온 전지는 배터리가 폐기될 때, 가장 위험한 폐기물 중 한가지를 발생시킨다. 스마트 카에 사용되는 리튬 이온 배터리는 우리가 일반적으로 사용하는 AA나 AAA배터리가 아니다. 그것들은 거대하다. 다 사용된 배터리는 쓰레기통에 버려질 것이고, 배터리 누수가 발생하면, 토양과 지하수에 곧바로 영향을 주게 된다. 배터리에서 산이 새어 나와 배터리를 둘러싼 모든 것이 영향을 받을 것이다. 따라서 AA 배터리에 비해 수백 배 더 큰 스마트 카 배터리의 경우, 그 영향은 훨씬 더 파괴적일 것이다.

ANSWERS AND SCRIPT

Actual Test 04

Page.168

00:10:00

당신의 교수님은 교육에 대한 수업을 하는 중이다.
교수님의 질문에 답하는 글을 쓰시오.

당신은 답변에서 다음을 수행해야 한다:
- 당신의 의견을 표현하고 지지한다
- 토론에 기여한다

유효한 응답에는 최소 100개의 단어가 포함된다.
당신은 그것을 쓸 시간이 10분 주어질 것이다.

쿠퍼 교수
최근 교육계의 동향에 대해 이야기해 보겠습니다. 이전에, 교실에는 의자와 테이블이 있는 물리적인 공간이 있었고, 학생들은 그들의 수업을 받기 위해 앉곤 했습니다. 오늘날, 가상 교실은 인터넷 덕분에 존재하고, 학생들은 컴퓨터 화면에 몰입하면서 집의 편안함을 배울 수 있습니다. 제 질문은 이것입니다. 온라인 수업의 영향에서 가장 중요한 것은 무엇입니까? 그리고 그 이유는 뭐죠?

페니
온라인 수업은 반 친구들과의 상호작용을 거의 불가능하게 만들었습니다. 신체적으로 수업을 듣는 것에 대한 가장 좋은 점 중 하나는 반 친구들과 할 수 있는 상호작용이었습니다. 이제 반 친구들이 온라인에서 만나기 때문에, 진정한 상호작용은 일어나지 않습니다. 문자 채팅이 가능하더라도, 교수님은 그 기능을 끌 수 있어서 반 친구들 사이의 어떠한 상호작용도 쓸모없게 만들 수 있습니다.

레너드
온라인 수업이 주는 가장 중요한 영향은 가상 도구를 사용하여 더 효과적인 수업을 허용하는 것입니다. 인터넷에는 교수들이 온라인 수업 중에 사용할 수 있는 많은 자원들이 있습니다. 재미있는 유튜브 비디오는 수업 시간에 학생들의 주의를 끄는 것을 돕고, 과학 실험이나 위험한 암시 때문에 학생들이 물리적인 교실에서 할 수 없는 다른 활동들을 자극하는 대화형 프로그램들이 있습니다. 예를 들어, 화학과 온라인 수업을 하는 동안, 제 교수님은 학교에서 사용할 수 없는 화학물질로 온라인 실험을 했고 심지어 다른 화학물질을 혼합함으로써 얼마나 큰 폭발이 일어날 수 있는지 보여주었습니다

Actual Test 04

통합 샘플 에세이
이 독서 지문은 스마트 자동차가 미래를 위한 몇 가지 이점을 가지고 있다고 주장한다. 하지만, 듣기 지문은 스마트 자동차가 미래에는 그렇게 유리하지 않을 것이라고 주장한다.

우선, 글쓴이는 스마트 자동차가 교통 흐름을 더 빠르게 하도록 도울 것이라고 주장한다. 스마트 카는 목적지에 도착하기 위해 가장 최적의 경로를 선택할 것이고, 따라서 이동 시간은 줄어들고 교통량은 줄어들 것이다. 또한 인간의 운전자는 운전 중 졸다가 사고를 낼 수 있고, 아마추어 운전자는 제한속도 이하로 운전하여 교통을 느리게 할 수 있기 때문에 운전 조건이 끊임없이 변화하기 때문에 스마트카는 교통에 도움이 되지 않을 것이라고 말하면서 이러한 주장을 반박한다. 스마트 자동차는 최적의 경로로 주행하는 동안 예상치 못한 사건에 직면할 것이다. 또한, 운전할 때 인간의 본능을 무시할 수 없다. 인간은 그들의 경험과 본능을 이용하여 그렇지 않았다면 골치아팠을 길을 피할 것이다.

게다가, 저자는 스마트 자동차는 유지비가 거의 들지 않을 것이라고 언급한다. 스마트 자동차는 무언가를 수리해야 할 경우 운전자에게 경고할 것이므로, 운전자는 비용이 많이 드는 정비가 되기 전에 문제를 해결할 수 있다. 스마트 자동차는 또한 자동차를 더 잘 다룰 것이고, 그래서 타이어, 엔진, 또는 브레이크 패드가 더 느리게 마모되어 수리에 소비되는 돈이 줄어들 것이다. 반대로, 강사는 스마트 카가 저렴하지 않을 것이라고 말하면서 이것에 반대한다. 스마트 자동차의 사소한 문제들을 고치는 것은 시장을 지배하지 않기 때문에 실제로 비용이 많이 든다, 그들의 부품과 수리는 가솔린 자동차보다 더 비쌀 것이다. 이 스마트 자동차는 한국에서 그렇게 인기가 없기 때문에 정비사들이 부품을 수입해야 할 수도 있다. 또한, 배터리를 교체하는 것은 자동차 그 자체만큼이나 비용이 많이 들 것이다. 도요타의 프리우스는 100달러 미만의 전통적인 자동차 배터리에 비해 만 달러 이상의 가치가 있는 배터리를 포함하고 있다.

게다가, 본문은 스마트 자동차가 휘발유가 아닌 리튬 이온 배터리로 작동한다고 주장한다. 이것은 유한한 자원인 화석 연료를 절약할 것이다. 또한, 배터리로 작동하는 자동차는 환경을 해치는 어떤 것도 방출하지 않기 때문에 스마트 자동차는 오염을 일으키지 않을 것이다. 반대로 스마트카의 리튬이온 배터리는 배터리가 방전될 때 위험한 폐기물이 발생한다는 내용으로 이 주장에 이의를 제기한다. 이러한 거대한 스마트 자동차 배터리에서 배터리 누출이 발생하면 토양과 지하수가 오염될 것이다. 산성 물질이 배터리 밖으로 새어나와 배터리 주변의 모든 것에 영향을 미친다. 그래서 실제로 스마트 자동차 배터리는 환경에 해를 입힌다.
429단어

학술 토론 샘플 에세이
수업은 더 이상 연필과 종이로 가르치지 않는다. 교육은 교사와 학생이 가상 교실 인에서 만날 수 있도록 발전했다. 비록 이 새로운 방법에는 많은 종과 휘파람이 있지만, 온라인 수업의 가장 중요한 영향은 학생들 사이의 게으름이다. 페니가 말했듯이, 학교에서 가장 좋은 기억 중 하나는 수업시간에 친구들과 이야기를 나누는 것이다. 온라인 수업이 그러한 개인적인 상호작용을 금지하는 만큼, 이것은 학생들이 그들의 관계에서도 게을러지게 만들었다. 친구를 직접 만나는 대신, 개인들은 외출 준비를 하는 것이 번거롭기 때문에 온라인에서 그들과 채팅하는 것을 선호한다. 게다가, 교수님은 학생들이 온라인 교실에서 주의를 기울이고 있는지조차 확인하지 않기 때문에 학생들은 온라인 수업을 빼먹기 쉽다. 어떤 사람들은 나중에 볼 수 있도록 누군가에게 강의를 녹음해 달라고 요청할 수 있기 때문에 심지어 온라인 강의에 참석하지 않을 수도 있다. 학생으로서, 그들은 수업이 온라인 강의실에 있더라도 그들의 강의를 따라가는 것에 대해 징계를 받아야 하고 책임을 져야 한다. 그러므로, 온라인 수업의 가장 큰 영향은 게으름이다.
190단어

Actual Test 05

Page.176

Reading

Question 1 of 2

요즘 소셜 미디어 계정이 없는 사람은 드물다. 소셜 미디어는 누구든지 보고 댓글을 달 수 있도록 사람들의 일상을 기록하고 보여준다. 소셜 미디어는 소속감을 높이고, 사회적 상호 작용을 만들며, 이를 이용하는 수 백만 명의 이용자들에게 취업 기회를 제공하는 데 도움이 된다는 데 동의하는 사람들이 많다.

소셜 미디어는 이용자들 사이의 소속감을 길러준다. 정치인이 시민들을 상대로 논쟁을 벌이거나 특정 사회 구성원들에게 피해를 줄 수 있는 법안의 통과를 장려할 때마다, 사람들은 함께 모여서 그들의 감정을 인터넷 상에서 공유할 것이다. 요즘 뉴스가 너무 빠르기 때문에 단 몇 초 만에 미국 동부 해안에서 온 사람들이 서부 해안에서 벌어지고 있는 부당함에 대해 알게 될 것이다. 소셜 미디어 이용자들은 같은 가치 아래 단결하고 그들의 네트워크는 사회에서 강한 목소리를 낼 것이다.

소셜 미디어에서는 사회적 상호 작용이 가능하다. 어떤 사람들은 대부분의 사람들처럼 다른 사람들과 정상적으로 의사소통을 할 수 없는 불안 문제를 가지고 있다. 소셜 미디어라는 베일 아래에서 이러한 사람들은 온라인 상의 친구를 사귈 수 있는데, 이는 컴퓨터 화면과 불안한 상호 작용으로부터 분리시켜주는 거리가 그들을 보호해 주기 때문이다. 또한, 온라인 상 사랑의 관계가 만들어질 수 있는데, 이는 요즘 사람들이 일 때문에 바쁜 나머지, 밖에 나가 로맨틱한 관계를 찾을 시간이 없기 때문이다. 지난 몇 년 동안, 데이트 사이트들은 로맨틱한 파트너들이 만나 성공적인 결혼을 할 수 있도록 만들어 주었다.

소셜 미디어에 의해 수 많은 일자리가 창출되었다. 페이스북과 같은 소셜 미디어 사이트는 단순한 인터페이스처럼 보일 수 있지만, 2020년 6월 현재 페이스북은 52,000명 이상의 사람들을 고용하고 있다. 이는 고급 소프트웨어 컴퓨터 회사인 마이크로소프트(MS)의 3분의 1에 가까운 수준이다. 게다가, 사람들은 구직 중인 사람들에게 채용 공고를 공유할 수 있다. 대부분의 기업은 고용 시장에 광고를 내는 대신 직원들이 추천하는 사람을 고용하는 것을 좋아한다. 직원이 SNS에 구인장을 게시하면 사람들은 그 게시물을 보고 희망을 안고 일자리를 얻을 수 있다.

Actual Test 05

Page.177

Listening

Question 1 of 2

(Female Professor)
Social media sites like Facebook, Instagram, and Tinder have been nothing but trouble since its development. Accounts have been hacked and cyber-crime has increased due to millions of users using it on a daily basis. Therefore, social media should not be promoted in society.

The idea that social media promotes a sense of unity is flawed. People coming together anonymously does not promote unity. When their true identities are hidden behind an anonymous user name, their opinions and actions do not matter. When push comes to shove, these social media users will not sign their names on petitions because they are afraid of showing their real identities in case the cause they are against backfires on them. The recent injustice displayed by police on George Floyd and the rise of Black Lives Matter is just one example. Facebook users would hashtag black lives matter and justice for George Floyd, but when it came down to going to court and appearing before a live jury, the number of people that showed up to support the case was not even half the number of users that voiced their opinions on Facebook.

Furthermore, social interactions that result from social media are actually lies. When individuals create their profiles on dating websites, they will often write fallacious information to make themselves more appealing to the opposite sex. Males will try to show off their masculinity by writing down sports as hobbies, when in fact they would rather sit on a sofa and play video games. Females would use photoshop to alter their profile pictures so that they can appear more aesthetic on the dating site. When these couples meet face to face, they will be left with disappointment, and will not trust the social interactions that arise from social media.

Moreover, jobs provided by social media are actually risky. When social media companies start, they will only hire a handful of employees. As the company grows, they may grab the attention from other companies that wish to buy out the company. When this happens, people will lose their jobs because the company that bought them out will transfer their employees to do the job. This actually happened when Facebook purchased Instagram. Hundreds of Instagram employees were laid off as Facebook employees took over. Also, job postings on social media sites can be uploaded by a con artist who wish to steal personal information from the naïve who upload their resume.

ANSWERS AND SCRIPT

페이스북, 인스타그램, 틴더와 같은 소셜 미디어 사이트들은 개발 이후 골칫거리가 되어 왔다. 계좌가 해킹되고 사이버 범죄는 수 백만 명의 사용자가 매일매일 사용함에 따라 증가했다. 그러므로 소셜 미디어는 사회에서 장려되어서는 안 된다.

소셜 미디어가 소속감을 높인다는 발상에는 결함이 있다. 익명으로 모인 사람들 사이에서는 단결이 도모되지 않는다. 익명의 사용자 이름 뒤에 그들의 진짜 정체성이 숨겨져 있을 때는, 그들의 의견과 행동은 문제가 되지 않는다. 결정적 순간이 왔을 때, 이런 소셜 미디어 이용자들은 탄원서에 서명을 하지 않는데, 이는 역효과가 날 경우를 대비해 자신의 실체가 드러나는 것을 두려워하기 때문이다. 최근 조지 플로이드 사건과 '흑인의 생명은 소중하다' 운동에서 보여준 경찰의 불의함이 하나의 예이다. 페이스북 이용자들은 흑인들의 생명 문제와 조지 플로이드에 대한 정의에 대해 해시태그 할 것이지만, 막상 법정에 소송을 제기하고 생방송 배심원단 앞에 나타나니, 그 사건을 지지하기 위해 모습을 드러낸 사람들의 숫자는 페이스북에서 의견을 개진한 사용자들의 절반도 채 되지 않았다.

게다가 소셜 미디어에서 이루어진다는 사회적 상호 작용은 사실 거짓말이다. 개개인이 데이트 웹사이트에 그들의 프로필을 만들 때, 종종 이성에게 더 어필하기 위해 잘못된 정보를 쓸 수 있을 것이다. 남성들은 스포츠를 취미로 적으면서 남성성을 과시하려고 할 것인데, 실제로는 소파에 앉아 비디오 게임을 하는 것을 더 좋아한다. 여성들은 데이트 사이트에서 더 예뻐 보이기 위해 포토샵을 사용하여 그들의 프로필 사진을 바꿀 것이다. 이러한 커플들은 직접 만나면 실망하게 될 것이고, 소셜 미디어에서 이루어지는 사회적 상호 작용은 더 이상 신뢰 받지 못할 것이다.

더구나 소셜 미디어에서 제공하는 일자리는 사실 위험하다. 소셜 미디어 기업들은 창업할 때, 소수의 직원만을 채용할 것이다. 기업이 성장함에 따라, 그 기업을 인수하기를 원하는 다른 기업들의 관심을 끌게 될 것이다. 이렇게 되면 사람들이 자기 직업을 잃게 될 것인데, 그들을 데려온 회사가 그 일을 하는 직원들을 교체할 것이기 때문이다. 이는 실제로 페이스북이 인스타그램을 사들이면서 벌어진 일이다. 페이스북 직원들을 인수하는 과정에서 인스타그램 직원 수백 명이 해고됐다. 또한, 순진하게 이력서를 내는 사람으로부터 개인 정보를 훔치려는 사기꾼이 SNS에 채용 공고를 올릴 수도 있다.

Actual Test 05

Page.182

00:10:00

당신의 교수님은 마케팅 수업을 하는 중이다.
교수의 질문에 답하는 글을 쓰시오.

당신의 답변에서 다음을 수행해야 한다:
- 당신의 의견을 표현하고 지지한다
- 토론에 기여한다

유효한 응답에는 최소 100개의 단어가 포함된다.
당신은 그것을 쓸 시간이 10분 주어질 것이다.

스틴슨 박사
회사들은 소비자들에게 광고하기 위해 다양한 방법을 사용해왔습니다. 요즘, 새로운 장소는 소셜 미디어 인플루언서라는 제품과 서비스를 광고하는 인기 있는 방법이 되었습니다. 인스타그램과 유튜브와 같은 소셜 미디어 플랫폼의 인기와 함께, 영향력 있는 사람들은 소비자들의 행동을 변화시켰습니다 그들이 소셜 미디어에 전시하는 제품이나 서비스. 이 새로운 마케팅 전략에 대해 어떻게 생각하십니까? 그리고 그 이유는 뭐죠?

마샬
저는 소셜 미디어 인플루언서가 실제로 소비자의 구매 행동에 영향을 준다고 생각하지 않습니다. 사람들은 자신의 필요와 선호도에 따라 결정하기 때문에 장점을 말하지 않고 제품이나 서비스를 객관적으로 평가할 수 있을 정도로 충분히 똑똑합니다. 또한, 많은 인플루언서들이 홍보를 위해 노력하고 있습니다 .다른 제품과 서비스, 그것은 소비자들에게 혼란을 줍니다.

릴리
저는 화장품이나 최신 기기를 구매할 때 소셜 미디어 인플루언서에게 의존합니다. 인플루언서들이 메이크업을 해보고 도움이 되는 팁을 제공해주기 때문에, 저는 그들이 최고의 제품과 바르는 방법에 대한 튜토리얼을 제공해줄 것이라고 믿습니다. 또한, 저는 기술자가 아니기 때문에 다양한 도구를 사용하는 인플루언시를 보여주는 유튜브 클립을 봅니다. 그들이 제품을 사용하는 것을 보고 나는 느낍니다. 무엇을 살지 선택하는 것이 더 편합니다.

Answers and Script

Actual Test 05

통합 샘플 에세이

독서 지문은 소셜 미디어가 사용자들에게 몇 가지 이점을 제공한다고 주장한다. 하지만, 듣기 지문은 소셜 미디어가 사회에서 홍보되어서는 안 된다고 주장한다.

우선, 글쓴이는 소셜 미디어가 사용자들 사이에 통일감을 가져온다고 주장한다. 소셜 미디어를 통해 뉴스는 나라의 한 쪽에서 다른 쪽으로 빠르게 전달된다. 소셜 미디어 사용자들은 단결하여 자신의 의견을 말할 수 있다. 반면에 화자는 사람들이 오는 것을 진술함으로써 이러한 주장을 반박한다. 익명으로 함께 한다고 해서 통일이 되는 것은 아니다. 사람들의 정체성이 숨겨져 있을 때, 그들의 의견과 행동은 중요하지 않다. 그들은 자신들의 신원이 밝혀질까 봐 청원서에 서명조차 하지 않을 것이다. 예를 들어, George Floyd 사건의 부당함 동안, 페이스북에서 그들의 의견을 옹호하는 사람들 중 절반도 이 사건을 지지하지 않았다.

또한, 저자는 소셜 미디어를 통해 소셜 상호 작용을 달성할 수 있다고 언급한다. 어떤 사람들은 불안 문제를 가지고 있기 때문에, 그들은 소셜 미디어를 사용하여 신경질적인 상호 작용을 겪지 않고도 온라인에서 친구를 사귈 수 있다. 또한, 사람들은 온라인에서 서로 만날 수 있기 때문에 로맨스는 매치될 수 있다. 그래서 그들의 바쁜 업무 시간 동안에도 연애 관계가 형성되어 결혼으로 이어질 수 있다. 반대로, 강사는 소셜 미디어에서 수행되는 사회적 상호작용은 거짓말이라고 말하면서 이에 반대한다. 개인들은 자신들을 더 매력적으로 만들기 위해 허구의 정보를 만들 것이다. 거짓으로 확인된 사람들이 실제 만났을 때, 그들은 실망할 것이다.

게다가, 본문은 많은 일자리가 소셜 미디어에 의해 창출된다고 주장한다. 유명한 소셜 미디어 사이트인 페이스북은 실제로 공학 회사인 마이크로소프트가 고용한 사람들의 세 배를 고용하고 있습니다. 또한, 기업들은 채용 공고에서 무작위로 채용하는 대신 직원들이 추천하는 사람들을 채용하는 것을 선호하기 때문에 소셜 미디어 사용자들은 채용 기회를 공유할 수 있다. 반대로, 이 강의는 소셜 미디어가 제공하는 일자리는 위험을 수반한다고 언급함으로써 이 주장에 이의를 제기한다. 소셜 미디어 회사가 성장하면 더 큰 회사에 인수될 가능성이 있다. 이런 일이 일어나면, 사람들은 그들의 삶을 잃게 될 것이다. 페이스북이 인스타그램을 구매하고 수백 명의 인스타그램 직원을 해고하는 것은 하나의 예에 불과하다. 또한, 소셜 미디어에 일자리를 게시하는 것은 사기꾼들이 이력서를 올리는 사람들의 개인 정보를 훔칠 것이기 때문에 위험할 수 있다.

402단어

독립 샘플 에세이

전통적인 광고 방식은 구식이 되었고 소비자들은 인플루언서에게 의존하는 경향이 있다.
그럼에도 불구하고, 소셜 미디어 인플루언서들이 아무리 제품과 서비스를 광고하려고 노력해도, 저는 그들이 하는 말을 절대 믿지 않을 것이다. 저는 소비자들이 제품이나 서비스를 구매할 가치가 있는지 스스로 판단할 수 있을 정도로 똑똑하다는 마샬의 의견에 동의한다. 요즘 소비자들은 그들이 사고 싶은 물건을 조사하기 위해 많은 노력을 한다. 그들은 비용과 품질 면에서 유사한 품목을 비교하는 데 며칠을 보낼 것이다. 저는 또한 소셜 미디어 인플루언서들을 믿어서는 안 된다는 것을 덧붙이고 싶다. 결국, 그들은 돈을 받고 있다. 제품이나 서비스를 광고하기 위해 회사에 의해, 그래서 그들은 상품의 긍정적인 측면에 대해서만 언급할 것이다. 비록 그들이 좋아하지 않는 것이 있다 하더라도, 그들은 광고를 위해 돈을 지불하는 회사를 만족시키기 위해 거짓말을 해야 할 것이다. 따라서 소셜 미디어 인플루언서를 활용하는 이 새로운 마케팅 전략을 신뢰해서는 안 된다.

167단어